Anthony Trollope

by *P. D. Edwards*
Senior Lecturer in English
University of Sydney

LONDON

ROUTLEDGE & KEGAN PAUL

First published 1968
by Routledge & Kegan Paul Limited
Broadway House, 68-74 Carter Lane
London, E.C.4

Printed in Great Britain
by Northumberland Press Limited
Gateshead

SBN 7100 6332 6 (C)
SBN 7100 6394 6 (P)

The Profiles in Literature Series

This series is designed to provide the student of literature and the general reader with a brief and helpful introduction to the major novelists and prose writers in English, American and foreign literature.

Each volume will provide an account of an individual author's writing career and works, through a series of carefully chosen extracts illustrating the major aspects of the author's art. These extracts are accompanied by commentary and analysis, drawing attention to particular features of the style and treatment. There is no pretence, of course, that a study of extracts can give a sense of the works as a whole, but this selective approach enables the reader to focus his attention upon specific features, and to be informed in his approach by experienced critics and scholars who are contributing to the series.

The volumes will provide a particularly helpful and practical form of introduction to writers whose works are extensive or which present special problems for the modern reader, who can then proceed with a sense of his bearings and an informed eye for the writer's art.

An important feature of these books is the extensive reference list of the author's works and the descriptive list of the most useful biographies, commentaries and critical studies.

B.C.S.

Contents

CONTENTS

Anthony Trollope—his life and works

Life and reputation

Though Anthony Trollope (1815-82) was born only four years after Thackeray, and three after Dickens, their fame was at its height long before his had even begun. His first novel, *The Macdermots of Ballycloran*, appeared in 1847, but it was another ten years before the early 'Barsetshire' novels and *The Three Clerks* (1858) began to make his name widely known. During his own lifetime, and for long afterwards, his reputation rested chiefly on the Barsetshire novels (1855-67), though it was enhanced by other works such as *Orley Farm* (1862), *Rachel Ray* (1863), and *Can You Forgive Her?* (1864). After the completion of the Barsetshire series his popularity gradually waned, but many of what are now thought his best novels had yet to appear (see Bibliography).

Until 1867 Trollope was an official in the Post Office, stationed for many years (1841-59) in Ireland, where several of his novels are set. He was also sent on Post Office business to the Middle East, the West Indies, and

North America, and later made private visits to Australia, New Zealand, and South Africa. His accounts of *The West Indies and the Spanish Main* (1859), *North America* (1862), *Australia and New Zealand* (1873), and *South Africa* (1878) are all classics of their kind, and he also wrote novels or short stories about all the countries he visited, both in Europe and in other continents. Another classic of its kind is his *Autobiography*, written in 1876 and published in 1883, shortly after his death.

In his own lifetime, and ever since, he has generally been ranked just below his greatest contemporaries, Dickens and George Eliot. This is partly because he wrote too much and too quickly, or at any rate too carelessly: no fewer than forty-seven published novels (as well as many other works) in less than forty years. The very best of his novels, however, are among the masterpieces of the greatest age of English fiction.

Works

Sending a copy of his *Rachel Ray* to George Eliot, Trollope remarked:

> You know that my novels are not sensational. In Rachel Ray I have attempted to confine myself absolutely to the commonest details of commonplace life among the most ordinary people, allowing myself no incident that would be even remarkable in every day life. I have shorn my fiction of all romance.
>
> (*Letters*, ed. Booth, p. 138)

At the time when these words were written, the so-called 'sensation novel'—the melodramatic tale of mystery, horror, and crime—was at the height of its vogue: its most noted exponents were Wilkie Collins (*The Woman in*

White, etc.), Mrs. Henry Wood (*East Lynne*), and Miss M. E. Braddon (*Lady Audley's Secret*), and its chief sources of inspiration—or so many critics felt at the time—were Dickens and the Brontës. *Rachel Ray* is an altogether different kind of novel and, although it is an extreme example, most readers probably thought, and still do think, of Trollope as a novelist who did, to an unusual extent, 'confine' himself to 'the commonest details of commonplace life' and 'shear' his fiction of 'all romance'; if he drew his inspiration from any contemporary novelist, it was from Dickens's great rival, Thackeray.

Even at this early stage of his career, however, Trollope had shown that he had no real aversion to 'romantic' or 'sensational' subjects. Though best known as the chronicler of uneventful lives in an imaginary county called Barsetshire—a citadel of traditional rural values always under threat from new ways, but always, in the end, holding its own against them—he had already written three 'Irish' novels (none of which lack exciting incident); one historical romance with a French setting; two novels about young men falling into misery, dissipation, and even crime in the sternly competitive arena of life in London; a modish but feeble satire on the latest methods of advertising; and a 'tragic' study of a lady in a typical 'sensational' situation—one in which she suffers the disgrace of having an early crime brought to light. In short, Trollope was, and remained, a restlessly experimental writer, constantly seeking fresh subjects and fresh settings.

Yet, however mistaken the widely-held view of him as essentially a 'domestic' novelist, one who largely restricts himself to 'every day life', it is true that his fiction is conspicuously unromantic and unsensational in its total effect. Despite their wide variety of subject-matter, their

3

frequent recourse to strange and remarkable happenings in exotic places, nearly all his novels have in common an unexcited, matter-of-fact quality. They take all 'sensations'—crimes, outbursts of violent passion, strange mental aberrations—in their stride. They delight in exposing the prosaic reality that so often underlies glamour and romance. Their big emotional moments are almost invariably succeeded by ironic letdown. They show little interest in what is inscrutable in human nature and in the workings of providence. Often, they make an ostentatious show of confiding in the reader to allay his anxiety about the future course of events. Trollope makes no bones about intruding into the novel in his own person, to praise or reprimand a character or even to share with the reader the problems that beset him in trying to tell his story clearly, fairly, and in chronological order. He likes to present himself to us as a man we can trust not to mislead us, a man whose one concern is to tell the truth with as little distortion as possible for 'artistic effect'. His novels, he would have us believe, are as true to life as novels can be—and to life as most of us know it.

Because of the very convincing illusion they produce of realism and ordinariness, their artfulness and artificiality are often overlooked. Even Trollope himself seems to have believed, part of the time at least, that their realism consisted mainly in the faithful reproduction of 'commonplace life', of what another critic called 'the familiar, the actual'. In his *Autobiography* (as well as in the novels themselves) he made much of his desire to create characters with whom the reader could identify himself, people who live as ordinary people do—'with not more of excellence, nor with exaggerated baseness'. Noble heroes and pitch-black villains would seem too

4

remote from the reader's own experience of life for him to be able to learn practical moral lessons from their behaviour and their successes and failures; and Trollope claimed that he attached much importance to the teaching of such lessons. In reality, however, he is likely to strike us as the least didactic of the great Victorian novelists; and if he was also—along with George Eliot—the most realistic, it wasn't simply because he confined himself to commonplace life. He did do this in some novels—as I have said—but in many others the fineness of his art is that it makes the extraordinary seem the ordinary, the exceptional seem the normal. In another passage of his *Autobiography*, he asserted that a 'good' novel must be 'both [realistic and sensational], and both in the highest degree'; by which he meant that it must take us outside everyday life, but still convince us that its world—no matter how different on the surface—is the world we know. This is what Trollope's art does. And it also, as a corollary, demonstrates the strangeness, both actual and potential, of what looks like familiar life. Like all art, it transforms and revitalises the 'life' that it depicts, making us see it in a new light; and it does so perhaps more deceptively and unobtrusively than the art of any other great English novelist, so deceptively indeed that it has often been mistaken for mere photography and denied the status of art at all.

Scheme of extracts

The passages below are designed to show that Trollope's 'realism' *is* the result of art—of sophisticated art—and to give an idea of the varieties of life, both familiar and strange, that it embodies. But they will also, I hope, reveal some of its weaknesses and some of the limitations of his style and imagination that his art disguises, but does not always conceal.

Extracts 1-5 illustrate some of the more obvious methods he uses to persuade us that what his novel presents— except in a few clearly-defined respects—is 'real life', or the closest imitation of real life that is possible in a novel.

Extracts 6, 7 and 8 offer typical examples of different kinds of 'realistic' character-portrayal.

The remaining passages, while giving further insight into Trollope's narrative style and its effects, have been chosen primarily to suggest something of the range of his subject-matter, with emphasis, naturally, on those subjects which he treats most distinctively.

PART ONE

Narrative method

The world of the novel and the real world

Trollope uses both real and imaginary settings for his novels. Of the real ones the commonest is London, where particular districts and even streets are frequently named. Of the imaginary settings the best known and most typical is Barsetshire, whose county town is Barchester. The two passages below are at the beginning and the end of the series of novels about Barsetshire.

I

The Rev. Septimus Harding was, a few years since, a beneficed clergyman residing in the cathedral town of ——; let us call it Barchester. Were we to name Wells or Salisbury, Exeter, Hereford, or Gloucester, it might be presumed that something personal was intended; and as this tale will refer mainly to the cathedral dignitaries of the town in question, we are anxious that no personality may be suspected. Let us presume that Barchester is a quiet town in the West of England, more remarkable for the beauty of its cathedral and the antiquity of its monuments, than for any commercial prosperity; that the west end of Barchester is the cathedral close, and that the aristocracy of Barchester are the bishop, dean, and canons, with their respective wives and daughters.

The Warden, ch. i (opening paragraph)

2

Before I take my leave of the diocese of Barchester for ever, which I purpose to do in the succeeding paragraph, I desire to be allowed to say one word of apology for myself, in answer to those who have accused me,— always without bitterness, and generally with tenderness,— of having forgotten, in writing of clergymen, the first and most prominent characteristic of the ordinary English clergyman's life. I have described many clergymen, they say, but have spoken of them all as though their professional duties, their high calling, their daily workings for the good of those around them, were matters of no moment, either to me, or in my opinion, to themselves. I would plead, in answer to this, that my object has been to paint the social and not the professional lives of clergymen; and that I have been led to do so, firstly, by a feeling that as no men affect more strongly, by their own character, the society of those around than do country clergymen, so, therefore, their social habits have been worth the labour necessary for painting them; and secondly, by a feeling that though I, as a novelist, may feel myself entitled to write of clergymen out of their pulpits, as I may also write of lawyers and doctors, I have no such liberty to write of them in their pulpits. When I have done so, if I have done so, I have so far transgressed. There are those who have told me that I have made all my clergymen bad, and none good. I must venture to hint to such judges that they have taught their eyes to love a colouring higher than nature justifies. We are, most of us, apt to love Raphael's madonnas better than Rembrandt's matrons. But, though we do so, we know that Rembrandt's matrons existed; but we have a strong belief that no such woman as Raphael painted ever did exist. In that he painted, as he may be surmised to have done, for pious purposes,—at least for Church purposes,—Raphael was justified; but had he painted so for family portraiture he would have been false. Had I written an epic about clergymen, I would have taken St. Paul for my model; but describing, as I have endeavoured to do, such clergymen as I see around me, I could not venture to be transcendental. For myself I can only say that I shall always be happy to sit, when allowed to do so, at the table of Archdeacon Grantly, to walk through the High Street of Barchester arm in arm with Mr. Robarts of Framley, and to stand alone and shed a tear beneath the modest black stone in the north transept of the cathedral on which is inscribed the name of Septimus Harding.

And now, if the reader will allow me to seize him affectionately by the arm, we will together take our last farewell of Barset and of the towers of Barchester. I may not venture to say to him that, in this country, he and I together have wandered often through the country lanes, and have ridden together over the too well-wooded fields, or have stood together in the cathedral nave listening to the peals of the organ, or have together sat at good men's tables, or have confronted together the angry pride of men who were not good. I may not boast that any beside myself have so realized the place, and the people, and the facts, as to make such reminiscences possible as those which I should attempt to evoke by an appeal to perfect fellowship. But to me Barset has been a real county, and its city a real city, and the spires and towers have been before my eyes, and the voices of the people are known to my ears, and the pavements of the city ways are familiar to my footsteps. To them all I now say farewell. That I have been induced to wander among them too long by my love of old friendships, and by the sweetness of old faces, is a fault for which I may perhaps be more readily forgiven, when I repeat, with some solemnity of assurance, the promise made in my title, that this shall be the last chronicle of Barset.

> *The Last Chronicle of Barset*, ch. lxxxiv
> (concluding paragraphs)

In the first of these passages Trollope says that Barchester might be any one of a number of real cathedral towns; in the second he insists that, to him at least, it and its people *have* been 'real', and he hopes that they will be equally so to the reader. Note his explanation for not having pictured the clergy (who comprise a large part of the cast of the Barsetshire novels) as 'transcending' ordinary humanity : if he had done this they would have seemed less 'real' because less familiar, less typical of their class; besides, they would not have been such good company for average men of the world like himself and the reader, men who accept and even have a certain fondness for each other's faults and for those of human nature in general. His central assumption—which is also the source of much of his characteristic humour—is that a 'realistic' view of human nature is one that shows clerical dignitaries, and indeed dignitaries in all walks of life, as having the same feet of clay, the same mundane preoccupations, the same sensitivity to mockery and other petty annoyances, as ordinary people like ourselves.

Some readers feel that a novelist shouldn't need to try

to convince us of the 'reality' of his characters and imaginary settings by proclaiming his own belief in it (as Trollope does in Extract ii); but it is a matter of opinion whether the practice is necessarily a confession of weakness.

Convention and realism

In his *Autobiography*, Trollope professed to believe that 'a good plot . . . is the most insignificant part of a tale', merely the 'vehicle' for the characters, who are the real centre of interest. As a result, he was often careless about the mechanics of his plots (though the best of them are quite intricate and have interesting 'ideas'). He liked at times to give the impression that his carelessness was deliberate, that it sprang from his conviction that the conventional 'good plot'—which readers expect and which, therefore, he must at least pretend to give them—is artificial and unrealistic. And in the same spirit he delighted in drawing attention to the absurdity of some accepted methods of story-telling.

3

Now we have come to our last chapter, and it may be doubted whether any reader,—unless he be some one specially gifted with a genius for statistics,—will have perceived how very many people have been made happy by matrimony. If marriage be the proper ending for a novel,—the only ending, as this writer takes it to be, which is not discordant,—surely no tale was ever so properly ended, or with so full a concord, as this one. Infinite trouble has been taken not only in arranging these marriages but in joining like to like,—so that, if not happiness, at any rate sympathetic unhappiness, might be produced. Our two sisters will, it is trusted, be happy. They have chosen men from their hearts, and have been chosen after the same fashion. Those two other sisters have been so wedded that the one will follow the idiosyncrasies of her husband, and the other bring her husband to follow her idiosyncrasies, without much danger of mutiny or revolt. As to Miss Docimer there must be room for fear. It may be questioned whether she was not worthy of a better lot than has been achieved for her by joining her fortunes to those of Frank Houston. But I, speaking for myself, have my hopes of Frank Houston. It is hard to rescue a man from the slough of luxury and idleness combined. If anything can do it, it is a cradle filled annually. It may be that he will yet learn that a broad back with a heavy weight upon it gives the best chance of happiness here below. Of Lord John's married prospects I could not say much as he came so very lately on the scene; but even he may perhaps do something in the world when he finds that his nursery is filling.

Ayala's Angel, ch. lxiv (final chapter)

4

Perhaps the method of rushing at once 'in medias res' is, of all the ways of beginning a story, or a separate branch of a story, the least objectionable. The reader is made to think that the gold lies so near the surface that he will be required to take very little trouble in digging for it. And the writer is enabled,—at any rate for a time, and till his neck has become, as it were, warm to the collar,—to throw off from him the difficulties and dangers, the tedium and prolixity, of description. This rushing 'in medias res' has doubtless the charm of ease. 'Certainly, when I threw her from the garret window to the stony pavement below, I did not anticipate that she would fall so far without injury to life or limb.' When a story has been begun after this fashion, without any prelude, without description of the garret or of the pavement, or of the lady thrown, or of the speaker, a great amount of trouble seems to have been saved. The mind of the reader fills up the blanks,— if erroneously, still satisfactorily. He knows, at least, that the heroine has encountered a terrible danger, and has escaped from it with almost incredible good fortune; that the demon of the piece is a bold demon, not ashamed to speak of his own iniquity, and that the heroine and the demon are so far united that they have been in a garret together. But there is the drawback on the system,—that it is almost impossible to avoid the necessity of doing, sooner or later, that which would naturally be done at first. It answers, perhaps, for half-a-dozen chapters;— and to carry the reader pleasantly for half-a-dozen chapters is a great matter!—but after that a certain nebulous darkness gradually seems to envelope the characters and the incidents. 'Is all this going on in the country, or is it in town,—or perhaps in the Colonies? How old was she? Was she tall? Is she fair? Is she heroine-like in her form and gait? And, after all, how high was the garret window?' I have always found that the details would insist on being told at last, and that by rushing 'in medias res' I was simply presenting the cart before the horse. But as readers like the cart the best, I will do it once again,— trying it only for a branch of my story,—and will endeavour to let as little as possible of the horse be seen afterwards.

The Duke's Children, ch. xi

The first of these passages illustrates two aspects of Trollope's style that have often been censured: the practice, complained of by the great novelist and critic Henry James, of 'reminding the reader that the story he was telling was only, after all, a make-believe' and that he 'could direct the course of events according to his pleasure'; and the habit of revealing, and inviting us to share, his own feelings towards his characters. Usually, when Trollope addresses us directly, he does so simply as the narrator, the teller of the tale. Here, however, he is doing what James objected to: admitting that he has invented it as well, that it is a 'make-believe'. What's more he seems to admit that it was made mechanically—not so much to reflect 'life' as to meet certain hypothetical specifications, by implication the conventional reader's. He claims to have taken 'infinite trouble' to pair off a large number of characters merely because marriage is the only 'proper' ending for a novel, or because, as he put it in *Barchester Towers*, 'The end of a novel, like the end of a children's dinner-party, must be made up of sweetmeats and sugar-plums'. Remarks like these occur chiefly in his more light-hearted novels and are a way of advising the reader not to take the novel too seriously, or at any rate not to take it as, in every respect, an imitation of real life. But, at the same time, by openly drawing our attention to elements in the novel's plot that are dictated by convention—that belong, by tradition, to novels, but do not belong to real life—he also implies that in most other respects the novel *can* be taken realistically. Though it is an extreme case, the passage highlights one important function of Trollope's repeated intrusions into his own novels: belonging both in the real world (our world) and in the novel, he is able to mediate between the two, showing us—sometimes explicitly, but most often implicitly—where they correspond and where they diverge. And his frequent expression of his own feelings about his characters—his own likes and dislikes, as well as his moral judgments—serves a similar purpose; for, as I noted in respect of Extract 2 they show that he himself thinks of them as 'real' people and expects us to do likewise.

In Extract 4, Trollope is intruding to discuss a problem in the art of story-telling; there is no suggestion this time that his story is in some respects a 'make-believe', rather than a 'true history' which he is merely passing on to us. You may feel that his problem is only a molehill out of which he is making a mountain, but he clearly has an ulterior aim: to let us see both the kind of story and the kind of story-telling that he finds uncongenial. As you will see, rushing 'in medias res' is the best way for a novelist to build up suspense, and it is characteristic of Trollope that he hardly ever resorts to it. Most often he prefers to project himself, though not always as openly as here, as a modest, confiding, almost bumbling fellow who wouldn't dream of trying to blind us with narrative science. Notice how the homely, hackneyed metaphors he uses contribute to this effect.

'Full confidence' between author and reader

In line with his belief that 'plot' is only a vehicle for 'character'—and by convention a rather wobbly, artificial one—Trollope liked to make a show of rejecting opportunities for 'suspense'. 'I abhor a mystery,' he exclaims in one of his novels (*The Bertrams*, Chapter 13); then proceeds to make a disclosure that in any case he could hardly have delayed any longer. And in *Barchester Towers* (Chapter 15), letting us in on a secret that we must in fact have guessed already, he expounds at some length his 'doctrine' of 'full confidence' between author and reader. Here is another example.

5

And now, O kind-hearted reader, I feel myself constrained, in the telling of this little story, to depart altogether from those principles of story-telling to which you probably have become accustomed, and to put the horse of my romance before the cart. There is a mystery respecting Mr. and Mrs. Peacocke which, according to all laws recognised in such matters, ought not to be elucidated till, let us say, the last chapter but two, so that your interest should be maintained almost to the end,—so near the end that there should be left only space for those little arrangements which are necessary for the well-being, or perhaps for the evil-being, of our personages. It is my purpose to disclose the mystery at once, and to ask you to look for your interest,—should you choose to go on with my chronicle,— simply in the conduct of my persons, during this disclosure, to others. You are to know it all before the Doctor or the Bishop,—before Mrs. Wortle or the Hon. Mrs. Stantiloup, or Lady De Lawle. You are to know it all before the Peacockes become aware that it must necessarily be disclosed to any one. It may be that when I shall have once told the mystery there will no longer be any room for interest in the tale to you. That there are many such readers of novels I know. I doubt whether the greater number be not such. I am far from saying that the kind of interest of which I am speaking,—and of which I intend to deprive myself,—is not the most natural and the most efficacious. What would the 'Black Dwarf' be if every one knew from the beginning that he was a rich man and a baronet? —or 'The Pirate', if all the truth about Norna of the Fitfulhead had been told in the first chapter.[1] Therefore, put the book down if the revelation of some future secret be necessary for your enjoyment. Our mystery is going to be revealed in the next paragraph,—in the next half-dozen words. Mr. and Mrs. Peacocke were not man and wife.

Dr. Wortle's School, ch. iii

Here Trollope makes a real and important disclosure, and makes it as early as possible in the novel. Moreover, the matter disclosed is one that most novels would surround with mystery and with wild emotion. For, as he goes on to tell us, Mr. and Mrs. Peacocke have committed

[1] *The Black Devil* and *The Pirate* are 'romantic' novels by Scott.

bigamy, going through a form of marriage in the mistaken belief that her husband had died; and bigamy was a favourite subject in the 'sensation novel' of Trollope's day (see above, pp. 2-3). It also occurs in no fewer than five of his own novels and usually occasions a degree of 'sensation'—violence, mystery, blackmail, long courtcases, etc. Nor is *Dr. Wortle's School* altogether an exception, since, as we soon discover, another mystery remains to be solved and can't be solved without danger. But, on the whole, the story as Trollope tells it is a good deal less exciting than most novelists, 'sensational' or otherwise, would have made it : even its most exotic scenes—involving some gun-toting in the Wild West of America—are described in Trollope's usual deadpan style.

From the passages we have looked at so far and those which follow, you should be able to judge how far, on balance, Trollope's authorial intrusions tend to enhance his novel's illusion of real life and how far to detract from it. Another matter worth considering is the extent to which Trollope, as narrator, assumes a 'persona' (or identity) distinct from his own, and the effect his doing so (or not doing so) has on our faith in the 'reality' of the imaginary world he creates.

The character sketch

As we have seen (Extract 4), Trollope preferred to describe his characters before showing them in action, and sometimes his initial descriptions of them are more interesting than their own subsequent behaviour. Perhaps because he believed, or thought he believed, that 'character' is more important than 'plot', his novels also contain many sketches, outline descriptions, of characters who play little or no part in the action.

6

He was a thin old man, who wore padded coats, and painted his beard and his eyebrows, and had false teeth, and who, in spite of chronic absence of means, always was possessed of clothes apparently just new from the hands of a West-end tailor. He was one of those men who, through their long, useless, ill-flavoured lives, always contrive to live well, to eat and drink of the best, to lie softly, and to go about in purple and fine linen,—and yet never have any money. Among a certain set Colonel Marrable, though well known, was still popular. He was good-tempered, well-mannered, sprightly in conversation, and had not a scruple in the world. He was over seventy, had lived hard, and must have known that there was not much more of it for him. But yet he had no qualms, and no fears. It may be doubted whether he knew that he was a bad man,—he, than whom you could find none worse though you were to search the country from one end to another. To lie, to steal,—not out of tills or pockets, because he knew the danger; to cheat—not at the card-table, because he had never come in the way of learning the lesson; to indulge every passion, though the cost to others might be ruin for life; to know no gods but his own bodily senses, and no duty but that which he owed to those gods; to eat all, and produce nothing; to love no one but himself; to have learned nothing but how to sit at table like a gentleman; to care not at all for his country, or even his profession; to have no creed, no party, no friend, no conscience, to be troubled with nothing that touched his heart;—such had been, was, and was to be the life of Colonel Marrable. Perhaps it was accounted to him as a merit by some that he did not quail at any coming fate. When his doctor warned him that he must go soon, unless he would refrain from this and that and the other,—so wording his caution that the Colonel could not but know and did know, that let him refrain as he would he must go soon,—he resolved that he would refrain, thinking that the charms of his wretched life were sweet enough to be worth such sacrifice; but in no other respect did the caution affect him. He never asked himself whether he had aught even to regret before he died, or to fear afterwards.

There are many Colonel Marrables about in the world, known well to be so at clubs, in drawing-rooms, and by the tradesmen who supply them. Men give them dinners and women smile upon them. The best of coats and boots are supplied to them. They never lack cigars nor champagne. They have horses to ride, and servants to wait upon them more obsequious than the servants of other people. And men will lend them money, too,—well knowing that there is no chance of repayment. Now and then one hears a horrid tale of some young girl who surrenders herself to such a one, absolutely for love! Upon the whole the Colonel Marrables are popular. It is hard to follow such a man quite to the end and to ascertain whether or no he does go out softly at last, like the snuff of a candle,—just with a little stink.

The Vicar of Bullhampton, ch. xxxiii

'There are many Colonel Marrables about in the world': he is, in other words, a type. In the action of the novel he plays only a subordinate part. His function is more to help set the scene than to act on it. He typifies a whole society, the society that tolerates and even likes him. The passage describes it as well as him, and does so with remarkable exactness and economy. It also epitomizes an important facet of Trollope's 'realism': that which depends on his easy assumption of the position of 'man of the world'; he too, we are made to feel, must have frequented clubs and drawing-rooms and dined-out among men who wear the 'best of coats and boots'.

Look closely at the *language* of the passage. How does it manage, with so few strongly emotive words, to express such disgust for Marrable and his type? 'Stink', you will notice, is so effective because it comes as a shock after the polite language of the rest of the passage.

Conversation, description and authorial commentary

Trollope, like most novelists, uses a combination of four ways of portraying character: he 'describes' it (as in the passage above), he sets down what his actors said and did on certain occasions, he summarizes what they were thinking and feeling at a given time (though usually without trying to represent their 'stream of consciousness', their actual thought-processes), and he 'comments' on their behaviour in order to explain it (or to admit that he can't) and to express or imply his own judgment of it. The next two passages show some of the characteristic effects he achieves by using all or some of these methods in a single scene.

7

(*Harry Clavering and Lady Ongar are tête à tête. They had formerly been in love with each other, but she had thrown Harry over to marry the wealthy Lord Ongar who had maltreated her and falsely accused her of being unfaithful to him. Now a widow, she is being persecuted by Count Pateroff and his sister Sophie Gordeloup, friends*

*of her late husband's. The count hopes to blackmail her
into marrying him by threatening to expose her alleged
—and in fact imaginary—misconduct during the period
of her marriage. Harry has recently become engaged to
Florence Burton, but Lady Ongar does not yet know this.
Harry is exclaiming at the wickedness of Count Pateroff.*)

'If what you surmise of him be true, he must be a very
devil. He cannot be a man—'

'Man or devil, what matters which he be? Which is the
worst, Harry, and what is the difference? The Fausts
of this day want no Mephistopheles to teach them guile or
to harden their hearts.'

'I do not believe that there are such men. There may be
one.'

'One, Harry! What was Lord Ongar? What is your
cousin Hugh? What is this Count Pateroff? Are they not
all of the same nature; hard as stone, desirous simply of
indulging their own appetites, utterly without one generous feeling, incapable even of the idea of caring for any
one? Is it not so? In truth this count is the best of the
three I have named. With him a woman would stand a
better chance than with either of the others.'

'Nevertheless, if that was his motive [*i.e., to blackmail
Lady Ongar into marrying him*], he is a devil.'

'He shall be a devil if you say so. He shall be anything
you please, so long as he has not made you think evil
of me.'

'No; he has not done that.'

'Then I don't care what he has done, or what he may
do. You would not have me see him, would you?' This
she asked with a sudden energy, throwing herself forward
from her seat with her elbows on the table, and resting
her face on her hands, as she had already done more
than once when he had been there; so that the attitude,
which became her well, was now customary in his eyes.

'You will hardly be guided by my opinion in such a matter.'

'By whose, then, will I be guided? Nay, Harry, since you put me to a promise, I will make the promise. I will be guided by your opinion. If you bid me see him, I will do it,—though, I own, it would be distressing to me.'

'Why should you see him, if you do not wish it?'

'I know no reason. In truth there is no reason. What he says about Lord Ongar is simply some part of his scheme. You see what his scheme is, Harry?'

'What is his scheme?'

'Simply this—that I should be frightened into becoming his wife. My darling bosom friend Sophie, who, as I take it, has not quite managed to come to satisfactory terms with her brother,—and I have no doubt her price for assistance has been high,—has informed me more than once that her brother desires to do me so much honour. The count, perhaps, thinks that he can manage such a bagatelle without any aid from his sister; and my dearest Sophie seems to feel that she can do better with me herself in my widowed state, than if I were to take another husband. They are so kind and so affectionate; are they not?'

At this moment tea was brought in, and Clavering sat for a time silent with his cup in his hand. She, the meanwhile, had resumed the old position with her face upon her hands, which she had abandoned when the servant entered the room, and was now sitting looking at him as he sipped his tea with his eyes averted from her. 'I cannot understand,' at last he said, 'why you should persist in your intimacy with such a woman.'

'You have not thought about it, Harry, or you would understand it. It is, I think, very easily understood.'

'You know her to be treacherous, false, vulgar, covetous, unprincipled. You cannot like her. You say she is a dragon.'

27

'A dragon to you, I said.'

'You cannot pretend that she is a lady, and yet you put up with her society.'

'Exactly. And now tell me what you would have me do.'

'I would have you part from her.'

'But how? It is so easy to say, part. Am I to bar my door against her when she has given me no offence? Am I to forget that she did me great service, when I sorely needed such services? Can I tell her to her face that she is all these things that you say of her, and that therefore I will for the future dispense with her company? Or do you believe that people in this world associate only with those they love and esteem?'

'I would not have one for my intimate friend whom I did not love and esteem.'

'But, Harry, suppose that no one loved and esteemed you; that you had no home down at Clavering with a father that admires you and a mother that worships you; no sisters that think you to be almost perfect, no comrades with whom you can work with mutual regard and emulation, no self-confidence, no high hopes of your own, no power of choosing companions whom you can esteem and love;—suppose with you it was Sophie Gordeloup or none,—how would it be with you then?'

His heart must have been made of stone if this had not melted it. He got up and coming round to her stood over her. 'Julia,' he said, 'it is not so with you.'

'But it is so with Julia,' she said. 'That is the truth. How am I better than her, and why should I not associate with her?'

'Better than her! As women you are poles asunder.'

'But as dragons,' she said smiling, 'we come together.'

'Do you mean that you have no one to love you?'

'Yes, Harry; that is just what I do mean. I have none to love me. In playing my cards I have won my stakes in money and rank, but have lost the amount ten times

28

told in affection, friendship, and that general unpro-
nounced esteem which creates the fellowship of men and
women in the world. I have a carriage and horses, and
am driven about with grand servants; and people, as they
see me, whisper and say that is Lady Ongar, whom nobody knows. I can see it in their eyes till I fancy that
I can hear their words.'

'But it is all false.'[1]

'What is false? It is not false that I have deserved this. I
have done that which has made me a fitting companion
for such a one as Sophie Gordeloup, though I have not
done that which perhaps these people think.'

He paused again before he spoke, still standing near her
on the rug. 'Lady Ongar—' he said.

'Nay, Harry; not Lady Ongar when we are together thus.
Let me feel that I have one friend who can dare to call
me by my name,—from whose mouth I shall be pleased
to hear my name. You need not fear that I shall think
that it means too much. I will not take it as meaning what
it used to mean.'

He did not know how to go on with his speech, or in
truth what to say to her. Florence Burton was still present
to his mind, and from minute to minute he told himself
that he would not become a villain. But now it had come
to that with him, that he would have given all that he
had in the world that he had never gone to Stratton [*where
Florence lives*]. He sat down by her in silence, looking
away from her at the fire, swearing to himself that he
would not become a villain, and yet wishing, almost wishing, that he had the courage to throw his honour over-
board. At last, half turning round towards her, he took her
hand, or rather took her first by the wrist till he could
possess himself of her hand. As he did so he touched her
hair and her cheek, and she let her hand drop till it rested

[1] Harry is referring to the allegation that she had been untrue
to her husband.

29

in his. 'Julia,' he said, 'what can I do to comfort you?'
She did not answer him, but looked away from him as she
sat, across the table into vacancy. 'Julia,' he said again,
'is there anything that will comfort you?' But still she did
not answer him.

He understood it all as well as the reader will understand it. He knew how it was with her, and was aware
that he was at this instant false almost equally to her and
to Florence. He knew that the question he had asked
was one to which there could be made a true and satisfactory answer, but that his safety lay in the fact that that
answer was all but impossible for her to give. Could she
say, 'Yes, you can comfort me. Tell me that you yet love
me, and I will be comforted?' But he had not designed
to bring her into such difficulty as this. He had not intended
to be cruel. He had drifted into treachery unawares, and
was torturing her, not because he was wicked, but because he was weak. He had held her hand now for some
minute or two, but still she did not speak to him. Then
he raised it and pressed it warmly to his lips.

'No, Harry,' she said, jumping from her seat and drawing her hand rapidly from him; 'no; it shall not be like
that. Let it be Lady Ongar again if the sound of the other
name brings back too closely the memory of other days.
Let it be Lady Ongar again. I can understand that it will
be better.' As she spoke she walked away from him across
the room, and he followed her.

'Are you angry?' he asked her.

'No, Harry; not angry. How should I be angry with you
who alone are left to me of my old friends? But, Harry,
you must think for me, and spare me in my difficulty.'

'Spare you, Julia?'

'Yes, Harry, spare me; you must be good to me and
considerate, and make yourself like a brother to me. But
people will know you are not a brother, and you must
remember all that for my sake. But you must not leave

me or desert me. Anything that people might say would be better than that.'

'Was I wrong to kiss your hand?'

'Yes, wrong, certainly wrong;—that is, not wrong, but unmindful.'

'I did it,' he said, 'because I love you.' And as he spoke the tears stood in both his eyes.

'Yes; you love me, and I you; but not with love that may show itself in that form. That was the old love, which I threw away, and which has been lost. That was at an end when I—jilted you. I am not angry; but you will remember that that love exists no longer? You will remember that, Harry?'

He sat himself down in a chair in a far part of the room, and two tears coursed their way down his cheeks. She stood over him and watched him as he wept. 'I did not mean to make you sad,' she said. 'Come, we will be sad no longer. I understand it all. I know how it is with you. The old love is lost, but we will not the less be friends.' Then he rose suddenly from his chair, and taking her in his arms, and holding her closely to his bosom, pressed his lips to hers.

He was so quick in this that she had not the power, even if she had the wish, to restrain him. But she struggled in his arms, and held her face aloof from him as she gently rebuked his passion. 'No, Harry, no; not so,' she said, 'it must not be so.'

'Yes, Julia, yes; it shall be so; ever so,—always so.' And he was still holding her in his arms, when the door opened, and with stealthy, cat-like steps Sophie Gordeloup entered the room. Harry immediately retreated from his position, and Lady Ongar turned upon her friend, and glared upon her with angry eyes.

'Ah,' said the little Franco-Pole, with an expression of infinite delight on her detestable visage, 'ah, my dears, is it not well that I thus announce myself?'

'No,' said Lady Ongar, 'it is not well. It is anything but well.'

'And why not well, Julie? Come, do not be foolish. Mr. Clavering is only a cousin, and a very handsome cousin, too. What does it signify before me?'

'It signifies nothing before you,' said Lady Ongar.

'But before the servant, Julie—?'

'It would signify nothing before anybody.'

'Come, come, Julie dear; that is nonsense.'

'Nonsense or no nonsense, I would wish to be private when I please. Will you tell me, Madame Gordeloup, what is your pleasure at the present moment?'

'My pleasure is to beg your pardon and to say you must forgive your poor friend. Your fine man-servant is out, and Bessy let me in. I told Bessy I would go up by myself, and that is all. If I have come too late I beg pardon.'

'Not too late, certainly,—as I am still up.'

'And I wanted to ask you about the pictures to-morrow? You said, perhaps you would go to-morrow,—perhaps not.'

Clavering had found himself to be somewhat awkwardly situated while Madame Gordeloup was thus explaining the cause of her having come unannounced into the room; as soon, therefore, as he found it practicable, he took his leave.

The Claverings, ch. xxi

What is perhaps most striking about this scene is that it is observed almost entirely from the outside, and with almost complete detachment. Speech, gestures, movements, and facial expressions are recorded in exact and (it appears) full detail, and for the most part without comment. At only one point are we taken inside the mind of either speaker: when we are told of Harry's awareness that he on the brink of treachery towards Florence and that he is 'torturing' Julia. In general, we have to infer their state of mind from outward evidence, above all from their speech. They are conversing, however, about a difficult and embarrassing subject, one about which words can never convey the whole truth and are very often a means of evading it. In addition, they both have special reasons for dissembling their feelings: Harry because of his engagement to Florence, and Julia because, having spurned Harry once, she must pretend to believe that she has forfeited her right to love or be loved by him now. (Her only hope is to lure him into reaffirming his love openly, which she does with some skill.) All or nearly all of the subtleties of the situation are conveyed purely by Harry's and Julia's speech. Notice especially the way she is made constantly to repeat the words that he himself has just used: by this means she makes it look as if he is guiding the conversation, whereas in fact she is; and she is also enabled to give her remarks a deceptively casual, listless air, befitting her pretence of dull despair. Notice, too, how both she and Harry slide into a slightly formal, stilted manner of expression when they are being insincere or deceiving themselves—how, for instance, her habitual 'Nay, Harry' becomes 'No, Harry' when she really means no, and how when he embraces her the falseness of his position is suggested by his hasty substitution of 'always so' for the more formal 'ever so'.

The dialogue and external 'description' of the scene are so effective as to make it questionable whether Trollope really needed to use other narrative methods at all. Could we not, for example, deduce for ourselves that Harry is doing his best not to 'become a villain', that he knows he is being 'false' to both his lovers but cannot help himself? Does Trollope's brief summary of his state of mind—

33

couched as it is in dispassionate language, remote from that of confused emotion—add anything to what we can deduce from Harry's spoken words? And is there not an air of special pleading in the authorial comment that Harry is not 'wicked' but merely 'weak'?

The scene's subject-matter is also interesting. Seductions are very rare in Trollope and are never described in detail. On this occasion one does seem imminent until Mme. Gordeloup arrives; but though many of Trollope's young men philander they nearly always stop short of fornication—or are stopped short by good (or ill) luck. In part this was no doubt a concession to Victorian squeamishness about sex; it also accords, however, with Trollope's rather ironical, unsensational view of life in general. He usually sees passion—sexual or other—in a faintly comic light, and he likes to build up (as he does here) towards a tremendous emotional crisis, then let the scene collapse into anti-climax. What could be more eloquently bathetic than the 'somewhat' in the last sentence of the passage quoted? Harry, it should be added, is among the weaker and shabbier of Trollope's young men, but like most of them is presented as an 'average', unheroic specimen of his class—neither better nor worse than most: the novel as a whole tends to endorse his own suspicion that, had he had more 'courage'—or at any rate, we may feel, more 'character'—he would have done the dishonourable thing and jilted Florence Burton in favour of Julia. That he even wishes he could do so is enough to explode his smug conviction—which Julia cannot talk him out of—that 'man' and 'devil' are altogether different species.

The crowd scene

Many of Trollope's characters are public men or leaders of fashionable society, and much of their private life is acted out on a public stage, with the gaze of the 'world' upon them. In the passage below he shows his mastery of the complex scene, in which a number of characters are involved, and in which action is occurring in several different places at once.

8

(*As a wealthy heiress, Lady Glencora had fallen in love with Burgo Fitzgerald, who had been fond of her but fonder still of her money. To save her from him, her guardians had dragooned her into marrying Plantaganet Palliser, a rising young politician and nephew of a duke. Now, Burgo, a handsome, personable, dissolute young aristocrat, is trying to persuade her to leave her husband and run away with him. The scene is a ball at the London home of Lady Monk, Burgo's aunt, who is privy to his project.*)

'Come and dance,' Lady Glencora said; 'I see a pair of eyes

looking at us.' The pair of eyes which Lady Glencora saw were in the possession of Mr. Bott, who was standing alone, leaning against the side of the doorway, every now and then raising his heels from the ground, so that he might look down upon the sinners as from a vantage ground. He was quite alone. Mrs. Marsham had left him, and had gotten herself away in Lady Glencora's own carriage to Park Lane, in order that she might find Mr. Palliser there, if by chance he should be at home.

'Won't it be making mischief?' Mrs. Marsham had said when Mr. Bott had suggested this line of conduct.

'There'll be worse mischief if you don't,' Mr. Bott had answered. 'He can come back, and then he can do as he likes. I'll keep my eyes upon them.' And so he did keep his eyes upon them.

Again they went round the room,—or that small portion of the room which the invading crowd had left to the dancers,—as though they were enjoying themselves thoroughly, and in all innocence. But there were others besides Mr. Bott who looked on and wondered. The Duchess of St. Bungay saw it, and shook her head sorrowing,—for the Duchess was good at heart. Mrs. Conway Sparkes saw it, and drank it down with keen appetite,— as a thirsty man with a longing for wine will drink champagne,—for Mrs. Conway Sparkes was not good at heart. Lady Hartletop saw it, and just raised her eyebrows. It was nothing to her. She liked to know what was going on, as such knowledge was sometimes useful; but, as for heart,—what she had was, in such a matter, neither good nor bad. Her blood circulated with its ordinary precision, and, in that respect, no woman ever had a better heart.[1] Lady Monk saw it, and a frown gathered on her brow. 'The fool!' she said to herself. She knew that Burgo

---

[1] Lady Hartletop and Mr. Palliser had once engaged in a tepid flirtation.

would not help his success by drawing down the eyes of all her guests upon his attempt. In the meantime Mr. Bott stood there, mounting still higher on his toes, straightening his back against the wall.

'Did you get my letter?' Burgo said again, as soon as a moment's pause gave him breath to speak. She did not answer him. Perhaps her breath did not return to her as rapidly as his. But, of course, he knew that she had received it. She would have quickly signified to him that no letter from him had come to her hands had it not reached her. 'Let us go out upon the stairs,' he said, 'for I must speak to you. Oh, if you could know what I suffered when you did not come to Monkshade [*his aunt, Lady Monk's, country house*]! Why did you not come?'

'I wish I had not come here,' she said.

'Because you have seen me? That, at any rate, is not kind of you.'

They were now making their way slowly down the stairs, in the crowd, towards the supper-room. All the world was now intent on food and drink, and they were only doing as others did. Lady Glencora was not thinking where she went, but, glancing upwards, as she stood for a moment wedged upon the stairs, her eyes met those of Mr. Bott. 'A man that can treat me like that deserves that I should leave him.'[2] That was the thought that crossed her mind at the moment.

'I'll get you some champagne with water in it,' said Burgo. 'I know that is what you like.'

'Do not get me anything,' she said. They had now got into the room, and had therefore escaped Mr. Bott's eyes for the moment. 'Mr. Fitzgerald,'—and now her words had become a whisper in his ear,—'do what I ask you. For the sake of the old days of which you spoke, the dear old days which can never come again—'

[2] She means her husband, who she believes has set Mr. Bott and Mrs. Marsham to spy on her.

'By G——! they can,' said he. 'They can come back, and they shall.'

'Never. But you can still do me a kindness. Go away, and leave me. Go to the sideboard, and then do not come back. You are doing me an injury while you remain with me.'

'Cora,' he said.

But she had now recovered her presence of mind, and understood what was going on. She was no longer in a dream, but words and things bore to her again their proper meaning. 'I will not have it, Mr. Fitzgerald,' she answered, speaking almost passionately. 'I will not have it. Do as I bid you. Go and leave me, and do not return. I tell you that we are watched.' This was still true, for Mr. Bott had now again got his eyes on them, round the supper-room door. Whatever was the reward for which he was working, private secretaryship or what else, it must be owned that he worked hard for it. But there are labours which are labours of love.

'Who is watching us?' said Burgo; 'and what does it matter? If you are minded to do as I have asked you——'

'But I am not so minded. Do you not know that you insult me by proposing it?'

'Yes;—it is an insult, Cora,—unless such an offer be a joy to you. If you wish to be my wife instead of his, it is no insult.'

'How can I be that?' Her face was not turned to him, and her words were half-pronounced, and in the lowest whisper, but, nevertheless, he heard them.

'Come with me,—abroad, and you shall yet be my wife. You got my letter? Do what I asked you, then. Come with me—to-night.'

The pressing instance of the suggestion, the fixing of a present hour, startled her back to her propriety. 'Mr. Fitzgerald,' she said, 'I asked you to go and leave me.

If you do not do so, I must get up and leave you. It will be much more difficult.'

'And is that to be all?'

'All;—at any rate, now.' Oh, Glencora! how could you be so weak? Why did you add that word, 'now'? In truth, she added it then, at that moment, simply feeling that she could thus best secure an immediate compliance with her request.

'I will not go,' he said, looking at her sternly, and leaning before her, with earnest face, with utter indifference as to the eyes of any that might see them. 'I will not go till you tell me that you will see me again.'

'I will,' she said in that low, all-but-unuttered whisper.

'When,—when,—when?' he asked.

Looking up again towards the doorway, in fear of Mr. Bott's eyes, she saw the face of Mr. Palliser as he entered the room. Mr. Bott had also seen him, and had tried to clutch him by the arm; but Mr. Palliser had shaken him off, apparently with indifference,—had got rid of him, as it were, without noticing him. Lady Glencora, when she saw her husband, immediately recovered her courage. She would not cower before him, or show herself ashamed of what she had done. For the matter of that, if he pressed her on the subject, she could bring herself to tell him that she loved Burgo Fitzgerald much more easily than she could whisper such a word to Burgo himself. Mr. Bott's eyes were odious to her as they watched her; but her husband's glance she could meet without quailing before it. 'Here is Mr. Palliser,' said she, speaking again in her ordinary clear-toned voice. Burgo immediately rose from his seat with a start, and turned quickly towards the door; but Lady Glencora kept her chair.

Mr. Palliser made his way as best he could through the crowd up to his wife. He, too, kept his countenance without betraying his secret. There was neither anger nor dismay in his face, nor was there any untoward hurry in his movement. Burgo stood aside as he came up, and Lady Glencora was the first to speak. 'I thought you were gone home hours ago,' she said.

'I did go home,' he answered, 'but I thought I might as well come back for you.'

'What a model of a husband! Well; I am ready. Only, what shall we do about Jane? Mr. Fitzgerald, I left a scarf in your aunt's room,—a little black and yellow scarf,— would you mind getting it for me?'

'I will fetch it,' said Mr. Palliser; 'and I will tell your cousin that the carriage shall come back for her.'

'If you will allow me—' said Burgo.

'I will do it,' said Mr. Palliser; and away he went, making his slow progress up through the crowd, ordering his carriage as he passed through the hall, and leaving Mr. Bott still watching at the door.

Lady Glendcora resolved that she would say nothing to Burgo while her husband was gone. There was a touch of chivalry in his leaving them again together, which so far conquered her. He might have bade her leave the scarf, and come at once. She had seen, moreover, that he had not spoken to Mr. Bott, and was thankful to him also for that. Burgo also seemed to have become aware that his chance for that time was over. 'I will say good night,' he said. 'Good night, Mr. Fitzgerald,' she answered, giving him her hand. He pressed it for a moment, and then turned and went. When Mr. Palliser came back he was no more to be seen.

Can You Forgive Her? ch. 1

This is a 'theatrical' scene, appropriate to the romantic and rather shallow characters of Burgo and Lady Glencora; but for all its tension and suppressed excitement it turns a completely blind eye to the romance of their situation, even imbuing it with a faintly ludicrous quality.

As in the last passage, most of the action is observed from without and with detachment: even what we are told about the feelings of the onlookers is deduced mainly from their facial expressions. At times, however, we are made to see the scene not so much as a detached observer would see it but as Lady Glencora sees it: Mr. Bott, for instance, is always observed from her angle of vision. We are also permitted to see into her mind, though again only intermittently and never very far; Burgo's mind, on the other hand, is completely closed to us. Most of what we are told that she is 'thinking' we could infer from her speech and her looks, but there is one crucial moment when, without the narrator's account of her motives, we should almost certainly misinterpret them—and, by doing so, judge her too harshly. To make quite sure that we do not, the narrator steps in and addresses her in his own person, asking the question that he no doubt feels the reader will ask. This is not the only occasion on which Trollope, by 'authorial commentary', lets his own sympathy for Lady Glencora and aversion for her enemies be seen: try to find the others for yourself. Do you think he would have done better to keep his feelings entirely to himself?

Can You Forgive Her?, from which this passage is taken, is the first of a series of novels in which Mr. Palliser (later Duke of Omnium) and his wife are leading characters. Palliser is a politician, and Mr. Bott and Mrs. Marsham are two of his political hangers-on: indeed, virtually all the people named in the passage are politically important to him. As the passage suggests, however, Trollope isn't interested in politics solely for its own sake; rather, he presents it as an aspect of social life—the 'high life' of fashionable London drawing-rooms and great country houses. Many of the characters in his 'semi-political tales' (as he called them) are indifferent to politics; but our interest in them is made more piquant by our awareness that the world they frequent is the world that governs the nation, as well as that of wealth and glamour (though also of ordinary and often very shabby human beings). This scene is highly characteristic in the way it intertwines political and private affairs, using each to enhance the interest of the other.

Judging by the present selection of extracts from his work, most of which are relevant in this connexion, you may feel that Trollope's most effective methods of portraying character are essentially superficial—in the sense that they generally restrict themselves to externally observable aspects of character. But you will make up your own mind whether this is a serious artistic shortcoming and how far it is the result of technical or imaginative limitations (or both) which Trollope fails to conceal.

PART TWO

Subject-matter

Love: the heroine

In most of Trollope's best novels the 'love interest' is subordinate to other interests. It was accepted—or so he chose to believe (compare Extract 3, above)—that 'there must be love in a novel'; and in his own it often seems to be included only in deference to convention. As a result, his love stories lack variety, and his lovers, though quite different from other novelists', show such a strong family likeness that once we have got to know a few of them the others are too predictable. In some of his early novels, however, they are portrayed with real freshness and psychological subtlety. He was especially noted, in his own day, for his 'girls'.

9

(*Lucy Robarts is speaking to her brother Mark's wife, Fanny, about her love for Lord Lufton.*)

'O heavens! what idiots we girls are! That a dozen soft words should have bowled me over like a ninepin, and left me without an inch of ground to call my own. And

I was so proud of my own strength; so sure that I should never be missish, and spoony, and sentimental! I was so determined to like him as Mark does, or you—'

'I shall not like him at all if he has spoken words to you that he should not have spoken.'

'But he has not.' And then she stopped a moment to consider. 'No, he has not. He never said a word to me that would make you angry with him if you knew of it. Except, perhaps, that he called me Lucy; and that was my fault, not his.'

'Because you talked of soft words.'

'Fanny, you have no idea what an absolute fool I am, what an unutterable ass. The soft words of which I tell you were of the kind which he speaks to you when he asks you how the cow gets on which he sent you from Ireland, or to Mark about Ponto's shoulder. He told me that he knew papa, and that he was at school with Mark, and that as he was such friends with you here at the parsonage, he must be good friends with me too. No; it has not been his fault. The soft words which did the mischief were such as those. But how well his mother understood the world! In order to have been safe, I should not have dared look at him.'

'But, dearest Lucy—'

'I know what you are going to say, and I admit it all. He is no hero. There is nothing on earth wonderful about him. I never heard him say a single word of wisdom, or utter a thought that was akin to poetry. He devotes all his energies to riding after a fox or killing poor birds, and I never heard of his doing a single great action in my life. And yet—' Fanny was so astounded by the way her sister-in-law went on, that she hardly knew how to speak. 'He is an excellent son, I believe,' at last she said.

'Except when he goes to Gatherum Castle. I'll tell you what he has: he has fine straight legs, and a smooth forehead, and a good-humoured eye, and white teeth. Was it possible to see such a catalogue of perfections, and not fall down, stricken to the very bone? But it was not that that did it all, Fanny. I could have stood against that. I think I could at least. It was his title that killed me. I had never spoken to a lord before. Oh, me! what a fool, what a beast I have been!' And then she burst out into tears. Mrs. Robarts, to tell the truth, could hardly understand poor Lucy's ailment. It was evident enough that her misery was real; but yet she spoke of herself and her sufferings with so much irony, with so near an approach to joking, that it was very hard to tell how far she was in earnest. Lucy, too, was so much given to a species of badinage which Mrs. Robarts did not always quite understand, that the latter was afraid sometimes to speak out what came uppermost to her tongue. But now that Lucy was absolutely in tears, and was almost breathless with excitement, she could not remain silent any longer. 'Dearest Lucy, pray do not speak in that way; it will all come right. Things always do come right when no one has acted wrongly.'

'Yes, when nobody has done wrongly. That's what papa used to call begging the question. But I'll tell you what, Fanny; I will not be beaten. I will either kill myself or get through it. I am so heartily self-ashamed that I owe to myself to fight the battle out.'

'To fight what battle, dearest?'

'This battle. Here, now, at the present moment I could not meet Lord Lufton. I should have to run like a scared fowl if he were to show himself within the gate; and I should not dare to go out of the house, if I knew that he was in the parish.'

'I don't see that, for I am sure you have not betrayed yourself.'

'Well, no; as for myself, I believe I have done the lying and the hypocrisy pretty well. But, dearest Fanny, you don't know half; and you cannot and must not know.'

'But I thought you said there had been nothing whatever between you.'

'Did I? Well, to you I have not said a word that was not true. I said that he had spoken nothing that it was wrong for him to say. It could not be wrong— But never mind. I'll tell you what I mean to do. I have been thinking of it for the last week—only I shall have to tell Mark.'

'If I were you I would tell him all.'

'What, Mark! If you do, Fanny, I'll never, never, never speak to you again. Would you—when I have given you all my heart in true sisterly love?' Mrs. Robarts had to explain that she had not proposed to tell anything to Mark herself, and was persuaded, moreover, to give a solemn promise that she would not tell anything to him unless specially authorized to do so.

'I'll go into a home, I think,' continued Lucy. 'You know what these homes are?' Mrs. Robarts assured her that she knew very well, and then Lucy went on: 'A year ago I should have said that I was the last girl in England to think of such a life, but I do believe now that it would be the best thing for me. And then I'll starve myself, and flog myself, and in that way I'll get back my own mind and my own soul.'

'Your own soul, Lucy!' said Mrs. Robarts, in a tone of horror.

'Well, my own heart, if you like it better; but I hate to hear myself talking about hearts. I don't care for my heart. I'd let it go—with this young popinjay lord or any one else, so that I could read, and talk, and walk, and sleep, and eat, without always feelings that I was wrong here—here—here—' and she pressed her hand vehemently against her side. 'What is it that I feel, Fanny? Why am I so weak in body that I cannot take exercise? Why cannot I keep my mind on a book for

one moment? Why can I not write two sentences together? Why should every mouthful that I eat stick in
my throat? Oh, Fanny, is it his legs, think you, or is it
his title?' Through all her sorrow—and she was very
sorrowful—Mrs. Robarts could not help smiling. And,
indeed, there was every now and then something even
in Lucy's look that was almost comic. She acted the irony
so well with which she strove to throw ridicule on herself! 'Do laugh at me,' she said. 'Nothing on earth will do
me so much good as that; nothing, unless it be starvation
and a whip. If you would only tell me that I must be a
sneak and an idiot to care for a man because he is good-
looking and a lord!'

'But that has not been the reason. There is a great deal
more in Lord Lufton than that; and since I must speak,
dear Lucy, I cannot but say that I should not wonder at
your being in love with him, only—only that—'

'Only what? Come, out with it. Do not mince matters,
or think that I shall be angry with you because you
scold me.'

'Only that I should have thought that you would have
been too guarded to have—have cared for any gentleman
till—till he had shown that he cared for you.'

'Guarded! Yes, that's it; that's just the word. But it's
he that should have been guarded. He should have had
a fire-guard hung before him, or a love-guard, if you
will. Guarded! Was I not guarded, till you all would
drag me out? Did I want to go there [*to Lord Lufton's
house*]? And when I was there, did I not make a fool
of myself, sitting in a corner, and thinking how much
better placed I should have been down in the servants'
hall. Lady Lufton [*Lord Lufton's mother*]—she dragged
me out, and then cautioned me, and then, then— Why
is Lady Lufton to have it all her own way? Why am I to be
sacrificed for her? I did not want to know Lady Lufton,
or any one belonging to her.'

49

'I cannot think that you have any cause to blame Lady Lufton, nor, perhaps, to blame anybody very much.'

'Well, no, it has been all my own fault; though, for the life of me, Fanny, going back and back, I cannot see where I took the first false step. I do not know where I went wrong.'

Framley Parsonage, ch. xxvi

Lucy does eventually marry Lord Lufton, as we have known all along that she will. Although Lord Lufton is her superior in rank and fortune, and although his mother is for a long time opposed to the match, it is clearly not a misalliance : for Lucy is a lady and Lord Lufton a gentleman, and in Trollope's eyes this makes them essentially equal. Our interest is in the growth and vicissitudes of their love, not in how their story will end. And, as is usually the case in Trollope, it is only a mildly remarkable love-affair, with little of the romance attaching to a grand passion or a scandalous misalliance.

Notice how completely Lucy is in command of the situation, despite her overwrought state. At one point we even find her promising not to be 'angry' with Fanny, though it is supposedly she who has misbehaved. Notice, too, how frankly she speaks of her love, even admitting that it is partly Lord Lufton's 'legs' she has fallen in love with. By Victorian standards, most of Trollope's heroines are very strong-minded and downright, and modern readers are likely to find them livelier and less insipid than most of their counterparts in, say, Dickens and Thackeray. In addition, they are often mentally and morally superior to their lovers, who tend (like Harry Clavering in Extract 7, above) to be callow, indiscriminately amorous, and a little bumptious—although as a sop to the Victorian male ego the heroines usually worship them as 'gods' nevertheless. Lucy is unusually free of illusions about her lover.

Look closely at Lucy's language : its vigorous slanginess and homeliness ('spoony', 'bowled me over like a nine-pin', 'run like a scared fowl') alternating with more formal speech, and its rather mannered, old-fashioned flavour ('popinjay lord', 'is it his legs, *think you*'). Lucy like many of Trollope's girls, is often praised for her 'naturalness', which in turn is seen as a tribute to Trollope's 'realism'; but in fact the illusion of naturalness, as this passage suggests, is artificially (and very skilfully) created. Much of the time Lucy talks and acts more like a Shake-spearean comic heroine (a Rosalind, a Viola, or a Beatrice) than a Victorian young lady, and in this she typifies the livelier of Trollope's girls.

Marriage without love

Trollope's love stories follow a largely conventional pattern. Lovers are, for a time, prevented from marrying either by parental disapproval, or by lack of money, or by discrepancies of rank or fortune; sometimes, one of the lovers mistakes his or her true feelings and forms another attachment which has to be broken before true love can triumph. In the end, however, all obstacles are removed and marriage results. It is an axiom, inseparable from this conventional kind of love story, that without love no marriage can be happy.

10

(Augustus Crosbie has jilted the heroine Lily Dale to marry the aristocratic Lady Alexandrina De Courcy. They have settled down in an ugly new house in an ugly new part of Bayswater, just within sight of Hyde Park.)

It was very dull. He was obliged to acknowledge to himself, when he thought over the subject, that the life which he was leading was dull. Though he could go into his club without annoyance, nobody there ever thought of asking him to join them at dinner. It was taken for granted that he was going to dine at home; and in the absence of any provocation to the contrary, he always did dine at home. He had now been in his house for three weeks, and had been asked with his wife to a few bridal dinner-parties, given chiefly by friends of the De Courcy family. Except on such occasions he never passed an evening out of his own house, and had not yet, since his marriage, dined once away from his wife. He told himself that his good conduct in this respect was the result of his own resolution; but, nevertheless, he felt that there was nothing else left for him to do. Nobody asked him to go to the theatre. Nobody begged him to drop in of an evening. Men never asked him why he did not play a rubber. He would generally saunter into Sebright's after he left his office, and lounge about the room for half an hour, talking to a few men. Nobody was uncivil to him. But he knew that the whole thing was changed, and he resolved, with some wisdom, to accommodate himself to his altered circumstances.

Lady Alexandrina also found her new life rather dull, and was sometimes inclined to be a little querulous. She would tell her husband that she never got out, and would declare, when he offered to walk with her, that she did not care for walking in the streets. 'I don't exactly see, then, where you are to walk,' he once replied. She did not tell him that she was fond of riding, and that the Park was a very fitting place for such exercise; but she looked it, and he understood her. 'I'll do all I can for her,' he said to himself; 'but I'll not ruin myself.' 'Amelia [*Lady Alexandrina's sister*] is coming to take me for a drive,' she said another time. 'Ah, that'll be very nice,' he answered. 'No; it won't be very nice,' said Alexandrina. 'Amelia is always shopping and bargaining with the trades-

people. But it will be better than being kept in the house
without ever stirring out.'

They breakfasted nominally at half-past nine; in truth,
it was always nearly ten, as Lady Alexandrina found it
difficult to get herself out of her room. At half-past ten
punctually he left his house for his office. He usually
got home by six, and then spent the greatest part of the
hour before dinner in the ceremony of dressing. He went,
at least, into his dressing-room, after speaking a few words
to his wife, and there remained, pulling things about,
clipping his nails, looking over any paper that came in his
way and killing the time. He expected his dinner punctually at seven, and began to feel a little cross if he were
kept waiting. After dinner, he drank one glass of wine in
company with his wife, and one other by himself, during
which latter ceremony he would stare at the hot coals,
and think of the thing he had done. Then he would go
upstairs, and have, first a cup of coffee, and then a cup of
tea. He would read his newspaper, open a book or two,
hide his face when he yawned, and try to make believe that
he liked it. She had no signs or words of love for him.
She never sat on his knee, or caressed him. She never
showed him that any happiness had come to her in being
allowed to live close to him. They thought that they loved
each other:—each thought so; but there was no love, no
sympathy, no warmth. The very atmosphere was cold;—
so cold that no fire could remove the chill.

In what way would it have been different had Lily
Dale sat opposite to him there as his wife, instead of
Lady Alexandrina? He told himself frequently that either
with one or the other life would have been the same; that
he had made himself for a while unfit for domestic life,
and that he must cure himself of that unfitness. But
though he declared this to himself in one set of half-spoken
thoughts, he would also declare to himself in another set,
that Lily would have made the whole house bright with her

54

brightness; that had he brought her home to his hearth, there would have been a sun shining on him every morning and every evening. But, nevertheless, he strove to do his duty, and remembered that the excitement of official life was still open to him. From eleven in the morning till five in the afternoon he could still hold a position which made it necessary that men should regard him with respect, and speak to him with deference. In this respect he was better off than his wife, for she had no office to which she could betake herself.

'Yes,' she said to Amelia, 'it is all very nice, and I don't mind the house being damp; but I get so tired of being alone.'

'That must be the case with women who are married to men of business.'

'Oh, I don't complain. Of course I knew what I was about. I suppose it won't be so very dull when everybody is up in London.'

'I don't find the season makes much difference to us after Christmas,' said Amelia; 'but no doubt London is gayer in May. You'll find you'll like it better next year; and perhaps you'll have a baby, you know.'

'Psha!' ejaculated Lady Alexandrina; 'I don't want a baby, and don't suppose I shall have one.'

'It's always something to do, you know.'

Lady Alexandrina, though she was not of an energetic temperament, could not but confess to herself that she had made a mistake. She had been tempted to marry Crosbie because Crosbie was a man of fashion, and now she was told that the London season would make no difference to her;—the London season which had hitherto always brought to her the excitement of parties, if it had not given her the satisfaction of amusement. She had been tempted to marry because it appeared to her that a married woman could enjoy society with less restraint than a girl who was subject to her mother or her chaperon;

that she would have more freedom of action as a married woman; and now she was told that she must wait for a baby before she could have anything to do. Courcy Castle was sometimes dull, but Courcy Castle would have been better than this.

When Crosbie returned home after this little conversation about the baby, he was told by his wife that they were to dine with the Gazebees on the next Sunday. On hearing this he shook his head with vexation. He knew, however, that he had no right to make complaint, as he had been only taken to St. John's Wood once since they had come home from their marriage trip. There was, however, one point as to which he could grumble. 'Why, on earth, on Sunday?'

'Because Amelia asked me for Sunday. If you are asked for Sunday, you cannot say you'll go on Monday.'

'It is so terrible on a Sunday afternoon. At what hour?'

'She said half-past five.'

'Heavens and earth! What are we to do all the evening?'

'It is not kind of you, Adolphus, to speak in that way of my relations.'

'Come, my love, that's a joke; as if I hadn't heard you say the same thing twenty times. You've complained of having to go up there much more bitterly than I ever did. You know I like your sister, and, in his way, Gazebee is a very good fellow; but after three or four hours, one begins to have had enough of him.'

'It can't be much duller than it is—;' but Lady Alexandrina stopped herself before she finished her speech.

'One can always read at home, at any rate,' said Crosbie.

'One can't always be reading. However, I have said you would go. If you choose to refuse, you must write and explain.'

The Small House at Allington, ch. xlviii

This is Trollope at his grimmest and most realistic. Every detail, both of the description and of the dialogue, plays its part in realizing two representative people in a representative situation. The art of the scene consists in its telling selection of detail—of nuances of speech and of fact; its absolute detachment (it is pure 'reportage', without any authorial comment); and, perhaps above all, its language. Trollope's level, regular style is ideal for expressing boredom—though it often fails with more active emotions. In different parts of the passage, the sense of monotony is conveyed almost as much by the simple, repetitive, nerveless sentence-structure and the repetition of key words ('dull', 'nobody', 'never', 'ceremony', 'punctually') as by the subject-matter. Note again the sparsity of 'emotive' words. When they are used the effect is for the most part one of hyperbole: as with Crosbie's 'terrible' and 'Heavens and earth', for example. Perhaps the most revealing word in the passage, however, is 'ejaculated', a rare departure from Trollope's usual, unemphatic 'said': can you see why he chooses the more emphatic word here?

The clergy: sacred

Trollope is probably best known for his many studies of clergymen. Most of these, as he says in Extract 2, above, show the clergy warts and all, in what he regards as the manner of Rembrandt. But occasionally the tone becomes more solemn, notably when Mr. Harding, the former warden of Hiram's Hospital, Barchester, or Mr. Crawley, the perpetual curate of Hogglestock, also in the diocese of Barchester, is the centre of attention. The passage below describes the death of Mr. Harding.

11

(*Archdeacon Grantly is married to one of Mr. Harding's daughters, Susan. Posy is one of the children of his other daughter, Eleanor—Mrs. Arabin. Mrs. Baxter is his house-keeper.*)

'I seem to have known him all my life,' said the arch-deacon. 'I have known him ever since I left college; and I have known him as one man seldom knows another. There is nothing that he has done,—as I believe, nothing

that he has thought,—with which I have not been cog-
nizant. I feel sure that he never had an impure fancy in
his mind, or a faulty wish in his heart. His tenderness has
surpassed the tenderness of woman; and yet, when occasion
came for showing it, he had all the spirit of a hero.
I shall never forget his resignation of the hospital, and
all that I did and said to make him keep it.'

'But he was right?'

'As Septimus Harding he was, I think, right; but it
would have been wrong in any other man. And he was
right, too, about the deanery.' For promotion had once
come in Mr. Harding's way, and he, too, might have been
Dean of Barchester. 'The fact is, he never was wrong.
He couldn't go wrong. He lacked guile, and he feared
God,—and a man who does both will never go far astray.
I don't think he ever coveted aught in his life,—except a
new case for his violoncello and somebody to listen to
him when he played it.' Then the archdeacon got up, and
walked about the room in his enthusiasm; and, perhaps,
as he walked some thoughts as to the sterner ambition
of his own life passed through his mind. What things had
he coveted? Had he lacked guile? He told himself that he
had feared God,—but he was not sure that he was telling
himself true even in that.

During the whole of the morning Mrs. Arabin and Mrs.
Grantly were with their father, and during the greater
part of the day there was absolute silence in the room. He
seemed to sleep; and they, though they knew that in truth
he was not sleeping, feared to disturb him by a word.
About two Mrs. Baxter brought him his dinner, and he
did rouse himself, and swallowed a spoonful of soup and
half a glass of wine. At this time Posy came to him, and
stood at the bedside, looking at him with her great wide
eyes. She seemed to be aware that life had now gone so far
with her dear old friend that she must not be allowed to sit
upon his bed again. But he put his hand out to her, and

she held it, standing quite still and silent. When Mrs. Baxter came to take away the tray, Posy's mother got up, and whispered a word to the child. Then Posy went away, and her eyes never beheld the old man again. That was a day which Posy never forgot,—not though she should live to be much older than her grandfather was when she thus left him.

'It is so sweet to have you both here,' he said, when he had been lying silent for nearly an hour after the child had gone. Then they got up, and came and stood close to him. 'There is nothing left for me to wish, my dears;—nothing.' Not long after that he expressed a desire that the two husbands,—his two sons-in-law,—should come to him; and Mrs. Arabin went to them, and brought them to the room. As he took their hands he merely repeated the same words again. 'There is nothing left for me to wish, my dears; —nothing.' He never spoke again above his breath; but ever and anon his daughters, who watched him, could see that he was praying. The two men did not stay with him long, but returned to the gloom of the library. The gloom had almost become the darkness of night, and they were still sitting there without any light, when Mrs. Baxter entered the room. 'The dear gentleman is no more,' said Mrs. Baxter; and it seemed to the archdeacon that the very moment of his father's death had repeated itself. When Dr. Filgrave called he was told that his services could be of no further use. 'Dear, dear!' said the doctor. 'We are all dust, Mrs. Baxter; are we not?' There were people in Barchester who pretended to know how often the doctor had repeated this little formula during the last thirty years.

There was no violence of sorrow in the house that night; but there were aching hearts, and one heart so sore that it seemed that no cure for its anguish could ever reach it. 'He has always been with me,' Mrs. Arabin said to her husband, as he strove to console her. 'It was not that I loved him better than Susan, but I have felt so much more of his loving tenderness. The sweetness of his voice has been in my ears almost daily since I was born.'

They buried him in the cathedral which he had loved so well, and in which nearly all the work of his life had been done; and all Barchester was there to see him laid in his grave within the cloisters. There was no procession of coaches, no hearse, nor was there any attempt at funereal pomp. From the dean's side door, across the vaulted passage, and into the transept,—over the little step upon which he had so nearly fallen when last he made his way out of the building,— the coffin was carried on men's shoulders. It was but a short journey from his bedroom to his grave. But the bell had been tolling sadly all the morning, and the nave and the aisles and the transepts, close up to the door leading from the transept into the cloister, were crowded with those who had known the name and the figure and the voice of Mr. Harding as long as they had known anything. Up to this day no one would have said specially that Mr. Harding was a favourite in the town. He had never been forward enough in anything to become the acknowledged possessor of popularity. But, now that he was gone, men and women told each other how good he had been. They remembered the sweetness of his smile, and talked of loving little words which he had spoken to them,— either years ago or the other day, for his words had always been loving. The dean [*Mr. Arabin*] and the archdeacon came first, shoulder to shoulder, and after them came their wives. I do not know that it was the proper order for mourning, but it was a touching sight to be seen, and was long remembered in Barchester. Painful as it was for them, the two women would be there, and the two sisters would walk together;—nor would they go before their husbands. Then there were the archdeacon's two sons,—for the Rev. Charles Grantly had come to Plumstead on the occasion. And in the vaulted passage which runs between the deanery and the end of the transept all the chapter, with the choir, the prebendaries, with the fat old chancellor, the precentor, and the minor canons down to the little choristers,—they all were there, and followed in at the transept door, two by two. And in the transept they were joined by another clergyman whom no one had expected to see that day. The bishop was there, looking old and worn,—almost as though he were unconscious of what he was doing. Since his wife's death no one had seen him out of the palace or of the palace grounds till that day. But there he was,—and they made way for him into the procession behind the two ladies,—and the archdeacon, when he saw it, resolved that there should be peace in his heart, if peace might be possible.

They made their way into the cloisters where the grave had been dug,—as many as might be allowed to follow. The place indeed was open to all who chose to come; but they who had only slightly known the man, refrained from pressing upon those who had a right to stand around his coffin. But there was one other there whom the faithful chronicler of Barchester should mention. Before any other one had reached the spot, the sexton and the verger between them had led in between them, among the graves beneath the cloisters, a blind man, very old, with a wondrous stoop, but who must have owned a grand stature before extreme old age had bent him, and they placed him sitting on a stone in the corner of the archway. But as soon as the shuffling of steps reached his ears, he raised himself with the aid of his stick, and stood during the service leaning against the pillar. The blind man was so old that he might almost have been Mr. Harding's father. This was John Bunce, bedesman from Hiram's Hospital,—and none perhaps there had known Mr. Harding better than he had known him. When the earth had been thrown on to the coffin, and the service was over, and they were about to disperse, Mrs. Arabin went up to the old man, and taking his hand between hers whispered a word into his ear. 'Oh, Miss Eleanor,' he said. 'Oh, Miss Eleanor!' Within a fortnight he also was lying within the cathedral precincts.

And so they buried Mr. Septimus Harding, formerly Warden of Hiram's Hospital in the city of Barchester, of whom the chronicler may say that that city never knew a sweeter gentleman or a better Christian.

The Last Chronicle of Barset, ch. lxxxi

Mr. Harding's death is of little importance in the plot of *The Last Chronicle of Barset*, but it is an appropriate finale to the Barsetshire novels as a whole. In earlier tales, and especially in *The Warden*, he has shown himself the choicest spirit among the clergy of Barset, refusing to be drawn into the bitter party feuds—'low church' against 'high church'—to which most of his colleagues devote themselves. As father-in-law of Archdeacon Grantly, leader of the high-church party, he had been accused of selling out to the enemy when, under pressure from reformers with a low-church bias, he resigned his wardenship. Now, however, even the archdeacon credits him with having shown 'all the spirit of a hero' in doing so; and at the time of his death he becomes an instrument of reconciliation, not only rousing the archdeacon to unwonted 'enthusiasm', and 'perhaps' to even more unwonted self-criticism, but also opening a prospect of 'peace' between him and his old enemy, the low-church Bishop Proudie, whose attendance at Mr. Harding's funeral softens the archdeacon's heart. Whether the promise of 'peace' will be realized is doubtful, but if it is Barchester will be a much less lively and amusing place: for the bellicosity and political zest of its priests, the eminently secular delight they take in their 'religious' wars, are one of the chief sources of vitality and humour in the Barset novels.

63

This being so, the passage above is perhaps open to a charge of sentimentality. Given that Mr. Harding has never been 'the acknowledged possessor of popularity', why should 'all Barchester' attend his funeral, and why should his 'goodness' and 'sweetness' be so much appreciated now when they weren't before? Is it likely that a very small child like Posy would 'never forget' her last sight of her grandfather, or that certain unconventional details of his funeral would be 'long remembered'? In Trollope's day, the ceremonial aspects of dying and burial were valued more highly than they are now: to die peacefully, bravely, and prayerfully was to prove one's Christian faith, and deathbeds and funerals offered both salutary warning and reassurance to the living. Even so, however, you may feel that in this passage the solemn concentration on externals —the solemnity broken only by the humorous reference to Dr. Filgrave's 'little formula'—enables Trollope to 'move' us without really bringing us face to face with death at all. The effect would be deeper if we were given some idea how the dying man feels—what it feels like to know one is dying —and if the onlookers thought less about Mr. Harding and more about death itself, including their own deaths.

The clergy: profane

The scene below takes place near another deathbed, that of Dean Trefoil of Barchester. It gives a more characteristic idea of Trollope's view of the clergy and of human nature in general.

12

(*Archdeacon Grantly is leader of the 'high-church' party in Barchester. The leaders of the 'low-church' party are Bishop Proudie and his formidable wife, and Mr. Slope, the bishop's chaplain.*)

The archdeacon alone of the attendant clergy had been admitted for a moment into the sick man's chamber. He had crept in with creaking shoes, had said with smothered voice a word of consolation to the sorrowing daughter, had looked on the distorted face of his old friend with solemn but yet eager scrutinising eye, as though he said in his heart 'and so some day it will probably be with me;' and then having whispered an unmeaning word or two to the doctors, had creaked his way back again into the library.

'He'll never speak again, I fear,' said the archdeacon as he noiselessly closed the door, as though the unconscious dying man, from whom all sense had fled, would have heard in his distant chamber the spring of the lock which was now so carefully handled.

'Indeed! indeed! is he so bad?' said the meagre little prebendary, turning over in his own mind all the probable candidates for the deanery, and wondering whether the archdeacon would think it worth his while to accept it. 'The fit must have been very violent.'

'When a man over seventy has a stroke of apoplexy, it seldom comes very lightly,' said the burly chancellor.

'He was an excellent, sweet-tempered man,' said one of the vicars choral. 'Heaven knows how we shall repair his loss.'

'He was indeed,' said a minor canon; 'and a great blessing to all those privileged to take a share of the services of our cathedral. I suppose the government will appoint, Mr. Archdeacon. I trust we may have no stranger.'

'We will not talk about his successor,' said the archdeacon, 'while there is yet hope.'

'Oh no, of course not,' said the minor canon. 'It would be exceedingly indecorous; but—'

'I know of no man,' said the meagre little prebendary, 'who has better interest with the present government than Mr. Slope.'

'Mr. Slope,' said two or three at once almost sotto voce. 'Mr. Slope dean of Barchester!'

'Pooh!' exclaimed the burly chancellor.

'The bishop would do anything for him,' said the little prebendary.

'And so would Mrs. Proudie,' said the vicar choral.

'Pooh!' said the chancellor.

The archdeacon had almost turned pale at the idea. What if Mr. Slope should become dean of Barchester? To be sure there was no adequate ground, indeed no ground at all, for presuming that such a desecration could even be contemplated. But nevertheless it was on the cards. Dr. Proudie had interest with the government, and the man carried as it were Dr. Proudie in his pocket. How should they all conduct themselves if Mr. Slope were to become dean of Barchester? The bare idea for a moment struck even Dr. Grantly dumb.

'It would certainly not be very pleasant for us to have Mr. Slope at the deanery,' said the little prebendary, chuckling inwardly at the evident consternation which his surmise had created.

'About as pleasant and as probable as having you in the palace,' said the chancellor.

'I should think such an appointment highly improbable,' said the minor canon, 'and, moreover, extremely injudicious. Should not you, Mr. Archdeacon?'

'I should presume such a thing to be quite out of the question,' said the archdeacon; 'but at the present moment I am thinking rather of our poor friend who is lying so near us than of Mr. Slope.'

'Of course, of course,' said the vicar choral with a very solemn air; 'of course you are. So are we all. Poor Dr. Trefoil; the best of men, but—'

'It's the most comfortable dean's residence in England,' said a second prebendary. 'Fifteen acres in the grounds. It is better than many of the bishops' palaces.'

'And full two thousand a year,' said the meagre doctor.

'It is cut down to £1200,' said the chancellor.

'No,' said the second prebendary. 'It is to be fifteen. A special case was made.'

'No such thing,' said the chancellor.

'You'll find I'm right,' said the prebendary.

'I'm sure I read it in the report,' said the minor canon.

'Nonsense', said the chancellor. 'They couldn't do it. There were to be no exceptions but London and Durham.'

'And Canterbury and York,' said the vicar choral, modestly.

'What do you say, Grantly?' said the meagre little doctor.

'Say about what?' said the archdeacon, who had been looking as though he were thinking about his friend the dean, but who had in reality been thinking about Mr. Slope.

'What is the next dean to have, twelve or fifteen?'

'Twelve,' said the archdeacon authoritatively, thereby putting an end at once to all doubt and dispute among his subordinates as far as that subject was concerned.

'Well, I certainly thought it was fifteen,' said the minor canon.

'Pooh!' said the burly chancellor. At this moment the door opened, and in came Dr. Fillgrave.

'How is he?' 'Is he conscious?' 'Can he speak?' 'I hope not dead?' 'No worse news, doctor, I trust?' 'I hope, I trust, something better, doctor?' said half a dozen voices all at once, each in a tone of extremest anxiety. It was pleasant to see how popular the good old dean was among his clergy.

Barchester Towers, ch. xxxi

There are various sources of humour in this scene. The most obvious is the way in which solemn, but conventionally parsonical, solicitude for the dying man struggles so ineffectually with solicitude—in every sense livelier—as to who will succeed him and what his successor will be paid. Apart from the archdeacon—at the beginning of the scene—nobody gives any thought either to death or to the dying man; and among clergymen such worldly indifference is bound to appear incongruous. Note, too, the amusing way in which the characters are differentiated by their

68

speech and, to some extent, by their clerical offices; also the quaint, almost liturgical effect produced by the repetition of their titles, which are their sole identifying marks. It can be argued that the scene has a double irony, showing up not only the worldliness of those who should be innocent, but also the innocence of their worldliness—perhaps of most worldliness.

If the previous passage was perhaps sentimental, is this one unnecessarily cynical?

Politics

In Extract 8 we saw how Trollope presents politics as, among other things, an exciting ingredient of social life—the life of 'high society'. He also believed that parliament itself, with its 'exciting changes', could offer 'all the keen interest of a sensational novel'. The passage below describes part of the debate on a Conservative measure to disestablish the Church of England. This measure, like the real-life Reform Bill of 1867, was against Conservative principles, but was designed to 'dish the Whigs' (the Liberals) by stealing one of their policies, then forcing them either to oppose it or, by supporting it, to help keep in office the minority Conservative government.

13

The galleries were crowded. Ladies' places had been ballotted for with desperate enthusiasm . . . Two royal princes and a royal duke were accommodated within the House in an irregular manner. Peers swarmed in the passages, and were too happy to find standing room. Bishops jostled against lay barons with no other preference than that afforded to them by their broader shoulders. Men, and especially clergymen, came to the galleries loaded with sandwiches and flasks, prepared to hear all there was to be heard should the debate last from 4 P.M. to the same hour on the following morning. At two in the afternoon the entrances to the House were barred, and men of all ranks,—deans, prebends, peers' sons, and baronets,—stood there patiently waiting till some powerful nobleman should let them through. The very ventilating chambers under the House were filled with courteous listeners, who had all pledged themselves that under no possible provocation would they even cough during the debate.

A few minutes after four, in a House from which hardly more than a dozen members were absent, Mr. Daubeny took his seat with that air of affected indifference to things around him which is peculiar to him. He entered slowly, amidst cheers from his side of the House, which no doubt were loud in proportion to the dismay of the cheerers as to the matter in hand. Gentlemen lacking substantial sympathy with their leader found it to be comfortable to deceive themselves and raise their hearts at the same time by the easy enthusiasm of noise. Mr. Daubeny having sat down and covered his head just raised his hat from his brows, and then tried to look as though he were no more than any other gentleman present. But the peculiar consciousness of the man displayed itself even in his constrained absence of motion. You could see that he felt himself to be the beheld of all beholders, and that he enjoyed the position,—with some slight inward trepidation lest the effort to be made should not equal the greatness of the occasion. Immediately after him Mr. Gresham bustled up the centre of the House amidst a roar of good-humoured welcome. We have had many Ministers who have been personally dearer to their individual adherents in the House than the present leader of the Opposition and late Premier, but none, perhaps, who has been more generally respected by his party for earnestness and sincerity. On the present occasion there was a fierceness, almost a ferocity, in his very countenance, to the fire of which friends and enemies were equally anxious to add fuel,—the friends in order that so might these recreant Tories be more thoroughly annihilated, and the enemies, that their enemy's indiscretion might act back upon himself to his confusion. For, indeed, it never could be denied that as a Prime Minister Mr. Gresham could be very indiscreet.

A certain small amount of ordinary business was done, to the disgust of expectant strangers, which was as trivial as possible in its nature,—so arranged, apparently, that the importance of what was to follow might be enhanced by the force of contrast. And, to make the dismay of the novice stranger more thorough, questions were asked and answers were given in so low a voice, and Mr. Speaker uttered a word or two in so quick and shambling a fashion that he, the novice stranger, began to fear that no word of the debate would reach him up there in his crowded back seat. All this, however, occupied but a few minutes, and at twenty minutes past four Mr. Daubeny was on his legs. Then the novice stranger found that, though he could not see Mr. Daubeny without the aid of an opera glass, he could hear every word that fell from his lips. . . .

A man destined to sit conspicuously on our Treasury Bench, or on the seat opposite to it, should ask the Gods for a thick skin as a first gift. The need of this in our national assembly is greater than elsewhere, because the differences between the men opposed to each other are smaller. When two foes meet together in the same Chamber, one of whom advocates the personal government of an individual ruler, and the other that form of State which has come to be called a Red Republic, they deal, no doubt, weighty blows of oratory at each other, but blows which never hurt at the moment. They may cut each other's throats if they can find an opportunity; but they do not bite each other like dogs over a bone. But when opponents are almost in accord, as is always the case with our parliamentary gladiators, they are ever striving to give maddening little wounds through the joints of the harness. What is there with us to create the divergence necessary for debate but the pride of personal skill in the encounter? Who desires among us to put down the Queen, or to repudiate the National Debt, or to destroy religious worship, or even to disturb the ranks of society? When some small measure of reform has thoroughly recommended itself to the country,—so thoroughly that all men know that the country will have it,—then the question arises whether its details shall be arranged by the political party which calls itself Liberal,—or by that which is termed Conservative. The men are so near to each other in all their convictions and theories of life that nothing is left to them but personal competition for the doing of the thing that is to be done. It is the same in religion. The apostle of Christianity and the infidel can meet without a chance of a quarrel; but it is never safe to bring together two men who differ about a saint or a surplice.

Mr. Daubeny . . . rushed boldly into the question of Church Reform, taking no little pride to himself and to his party that so great a blessing should be bestowed upon the country from so unexpected a source. 'See what we Conservatives can do. In fact we will conserve nothing when we find that you do not desire to have it conserved any longer. '*Quo nimium reris Graiâ pandetur ab urbe.*'[1] It was exactly the reverse of the complaint which Mr. Gresham was about to make. On the subject of the Church

[1] A misquotation of Vergil, *Æneid*, vi. 97: '[*Via prima salutis*,] *quod minime reris, Graiâ pandetur ab urbe.*' ('The first way of safety, though you least think so, will be revealed to you from a Greek city.') Similarly, in this case, those who seek reform will receive it from the supposed enemies of reform.

itself he was rather misty but very profound. He went
into the question of very early Churches indeed, and spoke
of the misappropriation of endowments in the time of Eli.
The establishment of the Levites had been no doubt complete; but changes had been effected as circumstances required. He was presumed to have alluded to the order of
Melchisedek, but he abstained from any mention of the
name. He roamed very wide, and gave many of his hearers
an idea that his erudition had carried him into regions in
which it was impossible to follow him. The gist of his
argument was to show that audacity in Reform was
the very backbone of Conservatism. By a clearly pro-
nounced disunion of Church and State the theocracy of
Thomas à Becket would be restored, and the people of
England would soon again become the faithful flocks of
faithful shepherds. By taking away the endowments from
the parishes, and giving them back in some complicated
way to the country, the parishes would be better able than
ever to support their clergymen. Bishops would be bishops
indeed, when they were no longer the creatures of a
Minister's breath. As to the deans, not seeing a clear way
to satisfy aspirants for future vacancies in the deaneries,
he became more than usually vague, but seemed to imply
that the Bill which was now with the leave of the House
to be read a second time, contained no clause forbidding
the appointment of deans, though the special stipend of the
office must be matter of consideration with the new
Church Synod.

The details of this part of his speech were felt to be dull
by the strangers. As long as he would abuse Mr. Gresham,
men could listen with pleasure; and could keep their attention fixed while he referred to the general Conservatism
of the party which he had the honour of leading. There was
a raciness in the promise of so much Church destruction
from the chosen leader of the Church party, which was
assisted by a conviction in the minds of most men that it

was impossible for unfortunate Conservatives to refuse to follow this leader, let him lead where he might. There was a gratification in feeling that the country party was bound to follow, even should he take them into the very bowels of a mountain, as the pied piper did the children of Hamelin;—and this made listening pleasant. But when Mr. Daubeny stated the effect of his different clauses, explaining what was to be taken and what left,—with a fervent assurance that what was to be left would, under the altered circumstances, go much further than the whole had gone before,—then the audience became weary, and began to think that it was time that some other gentleman should be upon his legs. But at the end of the Minister's speech there was another touch of invective which went far to redeem him. . . .

Phineas Redux, ch. xxxiii

Here, without apparent effort, Trollope achieves an impressive variety of effects. He communicates the excitement of a great parliamentary occasion, while at the same time exposing its absurd theatricality with cool precision. Though his attitude is satirical and debunking, he impresses us by his knowledge of Parliament (even down to the ventilation chambers), his understanding of its customs and procedures, his thoughtful and sympathetic definition of the relationship between its spirit and that of the country at large. He also, I think, makes us aware of his own political bias, yet appears quite detached. (Which party would you deduce that he himself supported?) He sees politics as a 'passion', which, like all passions, laughably exaggerates its own importance; but it is a passion that he clearly shares.

Daubeny was in most respects modelled on Disraeli, the real-life Conservative leader, and his Liberal opponent Gresham on Disraeli's real-life foe, Gladstone. There is clever parody of Disraeli—as well as of political double-talk in general—in the report of Daubeny's speech with its 'misty' analogies and its too-clever paradox that 'audacity in Reform is the very backbone of Conservatism'. The resemblances to real-life politicians and parallels to real-life political events would naturally have given the novel's original readers an added sense of realism and added excitement; but Trollope's satire still retains most of its pungency, and the 'passion' for politics that underlies it is still infectious.

Big business

Businessmen appear in a number of Trollope's novels. They are usually vulgar and snobbish, and often dishonest as well. In *The Way We Live Now*, widely regarded as his masterpiece, he pictured the old gentry, and especially the aristocracy, as selling out their possessions, their values, their very souls in order to share in the proceeds of shady commercial speculations; he also showed how their shabby example was being followed at every social level.

14

(Augustus Melmotte, a great financier of obscure but certainly foreign antecedents, is Conservative candidate for Westminster. He has been chosen to give a dinner for the visiting Emperor of China, and is now demanding an introduction to his prospective guest at a party they are both attending at the India Office. Lord Alfred Grendall, brother of a duke, is one of Melmotte's business associates and sponsors in 'society'. Mr. Wilson is Secretary of State for India, and therefore Melmotte's host on the present occasion, Lord De Griffin is an under-secretary at the India Office.

Mr. Longestaffe is an impoverished aristocrat who has found it convenient to let his London house to Melmotte.)

'By George, Alfred! I'm in earnest, and somebody had better look to it. If I'm not presented to his Imperial Majesty to-night, by G——, there shall be no dinner in Grosvenor Square on Monday. I'm master enough of my own house, I suppose, to be able to manage that.'

Here was a row. . . . Lord De Griffin was frightened, and Lord Alfred felt that something ought to be done. 'There's no knowing how far the pig-headed brute may go in his obstinacy,' Lord Alfred said to Mr. Lupton, who was there. It no doubt might have been wise to have allowed the merchant prince to return home with the resolution that his dinner should be abandoned. He would have repented probably before the next morning; and had he continued obdurate it would not have been difficult to explain to Celestial Majesty that something preferable had been found for that particular evening even to a banquet at the house of British commerce. The Government would probably have gained the seat for Westminster, as Melmotte would at once have become very unpopular with the great body of his supporters. But Lord De Griffin was not the man to see this. He did make his way up to Mr. Wilson, and explained to the Amphytrion of the night the demand which was made on his hospitality. A thoroughly well-established and experienced political Minister of State always feels that if he can make a friend or appease an enemy without paying a heavy price he will be doing a good stroke of business. 'Bring him up,' said Mr. Wilson. 'He's going to do something out in the East, isn't he?' 'Nothing in India,' said Lord Griffin. 'The submarine telegraph is quite impossible.' Mr. Wilson, instructing some satellite to find out in what way he might properly connect Mr. Melmotte with China, sent Lord De Griffin away with his commission.

'My dear Alfred, just allow me to manage these things myself,' Mr. Melmotte was saying when the under secretary returned. 'I know my own position and how to keep it. There shall be no dinner. I'll be d—— if any of the lot shall dine in Grosvenor Square on Monday.' Lord Alfred was so astounded that he was thinking of making his way to the Prime Minister, a man whom he abhorred and didn't know, and of acquainting him with the terrible calamity which was threatened. But the arrival of the under secretary saved him the trouble.

'If you will come with me,' whispered Lord De Griffin, 'it shall be managed. It isn't just the thing, but as you wish it, it shall be done.'

'I do wish it,' said Melmotte aloud. He was one of those men whom success never mollified, whose enjoyment of a point gained always demanded some hoarse note of triumph from his own trumpet.

'If you will be so kind as to follow me,' said Lord De Griffin. And so the thing was done. Melmotte, as he was taken up to the imperial footstool, was resolved upon making a little speech, forgetful at the moment of inter-preters,—of the double interpreters whom the Majesty of China required; but the awful, quiescent solemnity of the celestial one quelled even him, and he shuffled by with-out saying a word even of his own banquet.

But he had gained his point, and, as he was taken home to poor Mr. Longestaffe's house in Bruton Street, was intol-erable. Lord Alfred tried to escape after putting Madame Melmotte and her daughter into the carriage, but Melmotte insisted on his presence. 'You might as well come, Alfred;—there are two or three things I must settle before I go to bed.'

'I'm about knocked up,' said the unfortunate man.

'Knocked up, nonsense! Think what I've been through. I've been all day at the hardest work a man can do.' Had he as usual got in first, leaving his man-of-all-work to follow, the man-of-all-work would have escaped. Melmotte, fearing such defection, put his hand on Lord Alfred's shoulder, and the poor fellow was beaten. As they were taken home a continual sound of cock-crowing was audible, but as the words were not distinguished they required no painful attention; but when the soda water and brandy and cigars made their appearance in Mr. Longestaffe's own back room, then the trumpet was sounded with a full blast. 'I mean to let the fellows know what's what,' said Melmotte, walking about the room. Lord Alfred had thrown himself into an arm-chair, and was consoling himself as best he might with tobacco. 'Give and take is a very good motto. If I scratch their back, I mean them to scratch mine. They won't find many people to spend ten thousand pounds in entertaining a guest of the country's as a private enterprise. I don't know of any other man of business who could do it, or would do it. It's not much any of them can do for me. Thank God, I don't want 'em. But if consideration is to be shown to anybody, I intend to be considered. The Prince treated me very scurvily, Alfred, and I shall take an opportunity of telling him so on Monday. I suppose a man may be allowed to speak to his own guests.'

'You might turn the election against you if you said anything the Prince didn't like.'

'D— the election, sir. I stand before the electors of Westminster as a man of business, not as a courtier,—as a man who understands commercial enterprise, not as one of the Prince's toadies. Some of you fellows in England don't realize the matter yet; but I can tell you that I think myself quite as great a man as any Prince.' Lord Alfred looked at him, with strong reminiscences of the old ducal home, and shuddered. 'I'll teach them a lesson before long. Didn't I teach 'em a lesson to-night,—eh? They tell me that Lord De Griffin has sixty thousand a-year to spend. What's sixty thousand a-year? Didn't I make him go on my business? And didn't I make 'em do as I chose? You want to tell

me this and that, but I can tell you that I know more of
men and women than some of you fellows do, who think
you know a great deal.'

This went on through the whole of a long cigar; and
afterwards, as Lord Alfred slowly paced his way back to
his lodgings in Mount Street, he thought deeply whether
there might be a means of escaping from his present servi-
tude. 'Beast! Brute! Pig!' he said to himself over and over
again as he slowly went to Mount Street.

The Way We Live Now, ch. liv

In this scene Melmotte is drunk: when sober he generally shows a little more finesse. His success, however,
depends chiefly on the aggressiveness and ability to exude
confidence that he shows here. He lives on credit—not
only in the sense that most of his wealth is borrowed,
but also in the sense that his 'greatness', his legendary
capacity for making money, is merely an illusion in the eye
of a money-worshipping public. To sustain the faith of this
public he must project himself as a man for whom nothing is impossible. He is one of Trollope's finest charac-
terizations, and this scene suggests why. Notice how completely we are shut out of Melmotte's own consciousness.
We see and hear him almost exclusively as Lord Alfred
sees and hears him; we share Lord Alfred's impotent
horror. But all we see of him is his public presence, which
gives no indication of what has been hinted in a previous
scene: that he is on the brink of ruin and desperately
worried. Until his final moments, it is the same all the way
through: the novel deliberately presents him as primarily
a hollow, pasteboard figure, blown up to larger-than-life
size by the popular imagination. His abashed confronta-
tion with the Chinese emperor is a masterly piece of
irony; for the emperor, too, is a mere symbol, his 'majesty'

the product of illusion, of popular superstition, rather than his own individual qualities. But he at least is able to live up to his legend : Melmotte's brashness is a crude imitation of perfect self-confidence; the emperor's inscrutable repose is the real thing.

For the insight it offers into the interweaving of political and social life, and into the workings of the political mind, this passage invites comparison with Extract 14. It also provides a further illustration of Trollope's subtle sense of 'social tactics'.

Satire on rank

Though he is not blind to the glamour of 'high life', most of Trollope's aristocrats, statesmen, and church dignitaries are essentially very ordinary people. Lady Glencora Palliser, for example, whom we met in Extract 8, is perhaps the liveliest, most lifesize, and least pretentious duchess in English fiction. However, not all of Trollope's noble ladies —nor all of his statesmen and bishops—are above using the greatness of their rank to compensate for the littleness of their own natures.

15

There were two windows in the drawing-room wide open for the countess to pass through; but she saw that there was a woman on a sofa, at the third window, and that that woman had, as it were, a following attached to her. Her ladyship therefore determined to investigate the woman. The De Courcys were hereditarily short sighted, and had been so for thirty centuries at least. So Lady De Courcy, who when she entered the family had adopted the family habits, did as her son had done before her, and taking her glass to investigate the Signora Neroni, pressed in among the gentlemen who surrounded the couch, and bowed slightly to those whom she chose to honour by her acquaintance.

In order to get to the window she had to pass close to the front of the couch, and as she did so she stared hard at the occupant. The occupant in return stared hard at the countess. The countess who since her countess-ship commenced had been accustomed to see all eyes, not royal, ducal or marquesal, fall before her own, paused as she went on, raised her eyebrows, and stared even harder than before. But she had now to do with one who cared little for countesses. It was, one may say, impossible for mortal man or woman to abash Madeline Neroni. She opened her large bright eyes wider and wider, till she seemed to be all eyes. She gazed up into the lady's face, not as though she did it with an effort, but as if she delighted in doing it. She used no glass to assist her effrontery, and needed none. The faintest possible smile of derision played round her mouth, and her nostrils were slightly dilated, as if in sure anticipation of her triumph. And it was sure. The Countess De Courcy, in spite of her thirty centuries and De Courcy castle, and the fact that Lord De Courcy was grand master of the ponies to the Prince of Wales, had not a chance with her. At first the little circlet of gold wavered in the countess's hand, then the hand shook, then the circlet fell, the countess's head tossed itself into the air, and the countess's feet shambled out to the lawn. She did not however go so fast but what she heard the signora's voice, asking—

'Who on earth is that woman, Mr. Slope?'

'That is Lady De Courcy.'

'Oh, ah. I might have supposed so. Ha, ha, ha. Well, that's as good as a play.'

It was as good as a play to any there who had eyes to observe it, and wit to comment on what they observed.

But the Lady De Courcy soon found a congenial spirit on the lawn. There she encountered Mrs. Proudie, and as Mrs. Proudie was not only the wife of a bishop, but was also the cousin of an earl, Lady De Courcy considered her to be the fittest companion she was likely to meet in that assemblage. They were accordingly delighted to see each other. Mrs. Proudie by no means despised a countess, and as this countess lived in the county and within a sort of extensive visiting distance of Barchester, she was glad to have this opportunity of ingratiating herself.

'My dear Lady De Courcy, I am so delighted,' said she, looking as little grim as it was in her nature to do. 'I hardly expected to see you here. It is such a distance, and then you know, such a crowd.'

'And such roads, Mrs. Proudie! I really wonder how the people ever get about. But I don't suppose they ever do.'

'Well, I really don't know; but I suppose not. The Thornes don't, I know,' said Mrs. Proudie. 'Very nice person, Miss Thorne, isn't she?'

'Oh, delightful, and so queer; I've known her these twenty years. A great pet of mine is dear Miss Thorne. She is so very strange, you know. She always makes me think of the Esquimaux and the Indians. Isn't her dress quite delightful?'

'Delightful,' said Mrs. Proudie; 'I wonder now whether she paints. Did you ever see such colour?'

'Oh, of course,' said Lady De Courcy; 'that is, I have no doubt she does. But, Mrs. Proudie, who is that woman on the sofa by the window? just step this way and you'll see her, there—' and the countess led her to a spot where she could plainly see the signora's well-remembered face and figure.

She did not however do so without being equally well seen by the signora. 'Look, look,' said that lady to Mr. Slope, who was still standing near to her; 'see the high spiritualities and temporalities of the land in league together, and all against poor me. I'll wager my bracelet, Mr. Slope, against your next sermon, that they've taken up their position there on purpose to pull me to pieces. Well, I can't rush to the combat, but I know how to protect myself if the enemy come near me.'

But the enemy knew better. They could gain nothing by contact with the Signora Neroni, and they could abuse her as they pleased at a distance from her on the lawn.

'She's that horrid Italian woman, Lady De Courcy; you must have heard of her.'

'What Italian woman?' said her ladyship, quite alive to the coming story; 'I don't think I've heard of any Italian woman coming into the country. She doesn't look Italian either.'

'Oh, you must have heard of her,' said Mrs. Proudie. 'No, she's not absolutely Italian. She is Dr. Stanhope's daughter —Dr. Stanhope the prebendary; and she calls herself the Signora Neroni.'

'Oh-h-h-h!' exclaimed the countess.

'I was sure you had heard of her,' continued Mrs. Proudie. 'I don't know anything about her husband. They do say that some man named Neroni is still alive. I believe she did marry such a man abroad, but I do not at all know who or what he was.'

'Ah-h-h-h!' said the countess, shaking her head with much intelligence, as every additional 'h' fell from her lips. 'I know all about it now. I have heard George [*the countess's son*] mention her. George knows all about her. George heard about her in Rome.'

'She's an abominable woman, at any rate,' said Mrs. Proudie.

'Insufferable,' said the countess.

'She made her way into the palace once, before I knew anything about her; and I cannot tell you how dreadfully indecent her conduct was.'

'Was it?' said the delighted countess.

'Insufferable,' said the prelatess.

'But why does she lie on a sofa?' asked Lady De Courcy.

'She has only one leg,' replied Mrs. Proudie.

'Only one leg!' said Lady De Courcy, who felt to a certain degree dissatisfied that the signora was thus incapacitated. 'Was she born so?'

'Oh, no,' said Mrs. Proudie,—and her ladyship felt somewhat recomforted by the assurance,—'she had two. But that Signor Neroni beat her, I believe, till she was obliged to have one amputated. At any rate, she entirely lost the use of it.'

'Unfortunate creature!' said the countess, who herself knew something of matrimonial trials.

'Yes,' said Mrs. Proudie; 'one would pity her, in spite of her past bad conduct, if she now knew how to behave herself. But she does not. She is the most insolent creature I ever put my eyes on.'

'Indeed she is,' said Lady De Courcy.

'And her conduct with men is so abominable, that she is not fit to be admitted into any lady's drawing-room.'

'Dear me!' said the countess, becoming again excited, happy, and merciless.

Barchester Towers, ch. xxxvii

The comic detail in this scene is perfect: note particularly the way in which, in the description of Lady De Courcy's humiliation by the signora, attention is concentrated on her eye-glass and on the signora's eyes; the mocking hyperbole in 'thirty centuries at least'; the way in which the 'countess' and the 'prelatess' are made to repeat each other's words ('delightful', for example, and 'insufferable'); the sharp and subtle recording of Lady De Courcy's changing responses to the tale of the signora's missing leg—not least in the telling aside about her own 'matrimonial trials'.

The signora is one of Trollope's complete outsiders—people for whom the English social system, and most of its elaborate rules and taboos, have no meaning but are simply a source of irritation or (more often) of amusement. Consciously, Trollope himself was devoted to the system (though not to the obsessive pride of rank that distinguishes Lady De Courcy), but his imagination always comes brilliantly alive when identifying itself with the outsider's viewpoint. Other memorable outsiders are the signora's brother Bertie (in *Barchester Towers*), Mme. Gordeloup and Count Pateroff (cf. Extract 7 above), Mr. Scarborough (Extract 18), and in many respects Lizzie Eustace (Extract 17).

'Low life'

With only a few exceptions the leading characters in Trollope's novels are gentlefolk. The lower classes are usually relegated to comic subplots where they are treated less as recognizable human beings than as objects of 'fun'—most of it feeble and conventionally literary—for the socially superior reader. In particular, Trollope took delight—which even contemporary critics often found ill-natured—in mocking their efforts to ape the manners and customs of their betters. The passage below is unusually genial in spirit, and unusually fresh.

16

(*Mr. Tappitt is a small-town brewer, and Mrs. Butler Corn-bury lady of the nearby manor. 'Mrs. Rowan and Mary' are the mother and sister of a young gentleman who has inherited a share in the brewery. They are coming to stay with the Tappitts, and as they are 'ladies' Mrs. Tappitt plans a genteel party in their honour.*)

I am disposed to think that Mrs. Butler Cornbury did Mrs. Tappitt an injury when she with so much ready good-nature accepted the invitation for the party, and that Mrs. Tappitt was aware of this before the night of the party arrived. She was put on her mettle in a way that was disagreeable to her, and forced into an amount of submissive supplication to Mr. Tappitt for funds, which was vexatious to her spirit. Mrs. Tappitt was a good wife, who never ran her husband into debt, and kept nothing secret from him in the management of her household, —nothing at least which it behoved him to know. But she understood the privileges of her position, and could it have been possible for her to have carried through this party without extra household moneys, or without any violent departure from her usual customs of life, she could have snubbed her husband's objections comfortably, and have put him into the background for the occasion without any inconvenience to herself or power of remonstrance from him. But when Mrs. Butler Cornbury had been gracious, and when the fiddles and horn had become a fact to be accomplished, when Mrs. Rowan and Mary began to loom large on her imagination and a regular supper was projected, then Mrs. Tappitt felt the necessity of superior aid, and found herself called upon to reconcile her lord.

And this work was the more difficult and the more disagreeable to her feelings because she had already poohpoohed her husband when he asked a question about the party. 'Just a few friends got together by the girls,' she had said. 'Leave it all to them, my dear. It's not very often they see anybody at home.'

'I believe I see my friends as often as most people in Baslehurst,' Mr. Tappitt had replied indignantly, 'and I suppose my friends are their friends.' So there had been a little soreness which made the lady's submission the more disagreeable to her.

'Butler Cornbury! He's a puppy. I don't want to see him, and what's more, I won't vote for him.'

'You need not tell her so, my dear; and he's not coming. I suppose you like your girls to hold their heads up in the place; and if they show that they've respectable people with them at home respectable people will be glad to notice them.'

'Respectable! If our girls are to be made respectable by giving grand dances, I'd rather not have them respectable. How much is the whole thing to cost?'

'Well, very little T.; not much more than one of your Christmas dinner-parties. There'll be just the music, and the lights, and a bit of something to eat. What people drink at such times comes to nothing—just a little negus and lemonade. We might possibly have a bottle or two of champagne at the supper-table, for the look of the thing.'

'Champagne!' exclaimed the brewer. He had never yet incurred the cost of a bottle of champagne within his own house, though he thought nothing of it at public dinners. The idea was too much for him; and Mrs. Tappitt, feeling how the ground lay, gave that up,—at any rate for the present. She gave up the champagne; but in abandoning that, she obtained the marital sanction, a quasi sanction which he was too honourable as a husband afterwards to repudiate, for the music and the eatables. Mrs. Tappitt knew that she had done well, and prepared for his dinner that day a beefsteak pie, made with her own hands. Tappitt was not altogether a dull man, and understood these little signs. 'Ah,' said he, 'I wonder how much that pie is to cost me?'

'Oh, T., how can you say such things! As if you didn't have beefsteak pie as often as it's good for you.' The pie, however, had its effect, as also did the exceeding 'boilishness' of the water which was brought in for his gin-toddy that night; and it was known throughout the establishment that papa was in a good humour, and that mamma had been very clever.

'The girls must have had new dresses anyway before the

month was out,' Mrs. Tappitt said to her husband the next morning before he had left the conjugal chamber.

'Do you mean to say that they're to have gowns made on purpose for this party?' said the brewer; and it seemed by the tone of his voice that the hot gin and water had lost its kindly effects.

'My dear, they must be dressed, you know. I'm sure no girls in Baslehurst cost less in the way of finery. In the ordinary way they'd have had new frocks almost immediately.'

'Bother!' Mr. Tappitt was shaving just at this moment, and dashed aside his razor for a moment to utter this one word. He intended to signify how perfectly well he was aware that a muslin frock prepared for an evening party would not fill the place of a substantial morning dress.

'Well, my dear, I'm sure the girls ain't unreasonable; nor am I. Five-and-thirty shillings apiece for them would do it all. And I shan't want anything myself this year in September.' Now Mr. Tappitt, who was a man of sentiment, always gave his wife some costly article of raiment on the 1st of September, calling her his partridge and his bird,—for on that day they had been married. Mrs. Tappitt had frequently offered to intromit the ceremony when calling upon his generosity for other purposes, but the September gift had always been forthcoming.

'Will thirty-five shillings a-piece do it?' said he, turning round with his face all covered with lather. Then again he went to work with his razor just under his right ear.

'Well, yes; I think it will. Two pounds each for the three shall do it, anyway.'

Mr. Tappitt gave a little jump at this increased demand for fifteen shillings, and not being in a good position for jumping, encountered an unpleasant accident, and uttered a somewhat vehement exclamation. 'There,' said he, 'now I've cut myself, and it's your fault. Oh dear; oh dear!

When I cut myself there it never stops. It's no good doing that, Margaret; it only makes it worse. There; now you've got the soap and blood all down inside my shirt.'

Rachel Ray, ch. vi

This little tableau offers an extreme example of what Trollope means by the 'commonest details of commonplace life' (see above, p. 2). It impresses not only by its realistic detail, but also by its sheer informality. Shaving is one of a man's most private and undignified activities; so too is his financial bargaining with his wife. Yet Trollope makes both activities a normal, unremarkable part of his novel—as probably no other Victorian novelist could do so easily. (In another of his novels we overhear a bishop's wife nagging her husband on the nuptial bed as he tries to go to sleep.)

The Tappitts are lower middle-class, and part of the humour of the scene attaches to their class peculiarities: for example, the 'quaint' expressions they occasionally use ('respectable', 'T', 'boilishness'), Mr. Tappitt's fondness for gin-toddy (generally a lower-class drink), the openness and even zest with which they haggle over money (which more 'genteel' people would pretend to regard as a distasteful subject). In essence, however, the scene's comic subject is marriage in general rather than lower middle-class foibles in particular, and the foibles are not given the disproportionate stress that Trollope often does give them.

The rogue heroine

'Is it not a pity,' Trollope asks in *Barchester Towers*, 'that people who are bright and clever should so often be exceedingly improper?' I have mentioned the Signora Neroni as a case in point (Extract 15). But the most fully and subtly drawn of Trollope's 'rogues' are Lizzie Eustace and Mr. Scarborough. Neither is presented literally as a 'hero' or 'heroine' in the sense of being held up for moral approval; but both win our—and the author's—admiration by their vitality and mental resourcefulness, and their offences against conventional morality are often a condemnation as much of the conventionally moral as of themselves.

17

(Lizzie has illegally retained possession of a valuable diamond necklace, which she claims her late husband, Sir Florian Eustace, had 'given' her, and which his family, through their lawyer Mr. Camperdown, are now trying to make her give up. Her cousin Frank Greystock, en-

*gaged to Lucy Morris but infatuated with Lizzie, has
foolishly taken Lizzie's side.)*

She had been a very clever child,—a clever, crafty child;
and now she was becoming a clever woman. Her craft remained with her; but so keen was her outlook upon the
world, that she was beginning to perceive that craft, let it
be never so crafty, will in the long run miss its own object.
She actually envied the simplicity of Lucy Morris, for
whom she delighted to find evil names, calling her demure,
a prig, a sly puss, and so on. But she could see,—or half
see,—that Lucy with her simplicity was stronger than was
she with her craft. She had nearly captivated Frank Greystock with her wiles, but without any wiles Lucy had
captivated him altogether. And a man captivated by
wiles was only captivated for a time, whereas a man won
by simplicity would be won for ever,—if he himself were
worth the winning. And this, too, she felt,—that let her success be what it might, she could not be happy unless she
could win a man's heart. She had won Sir Florian's, but
that had been for an hour,—for a month or two. And then
Sir Florian had never really won hers. Could not she be
simple? Could not she act simplicity so well that the
thing acted should be as powerful as the thing itself;—
perhaps even more powerful? Poor Lizzie Eustace! In
thinking over all this, she saw a great deal. It was wonderful that she should see so much and tell herself so many
home truths. But there was one truth she could not see,
and therefore could not tell it to herself. She had not
a heart to give. . . .

Her ladyship had now come down to her country house,
leaving London and all its charms before the end of the
season, actuated by various motives. In the first place, the
house in Mount Street was taken, furnished, by the month,
and the servants were hired after the same fashion, and
the horses jobbed. Lady Eustace was already sufficiently

intimate with her accounts to know that she would save two hundred pounds by not remaining another month or three weeks in London, and sufficiently observant of her own affairs to have perceived that such saving was needed. And then it appeared to her that her battle with Lord Fawn could be better fought from a distance than at close quarters.[1] London, too, was becoming absolutely distasteful to her. There were many things there that tended to make her unhappy, and so few that she could enjoy! She was afraid of Mr. Camperdown, and ever on the rack lest some dreadful thing should come upon her in respect of the necklace,—some horrible paper served upon her from a magistrate, ordering her appearance at Newgate, or perhaps before the Lord Chancellor, or a visit from policemen, who would be empowered to search for and carry off the iron box. And then there was so little in her London life to gratify her! It is pleasant to win in a fight;—but to be always fighting is not pleasant. Except in those moments, few and far between, in which she was alone with her cousin Frank,—and perhaps in those other moments in which she wore her diamonds,—she had but little in London that she enjoyed. She still thought that a time would come when it would be otherwise. Under these influences she had actually made herself believe that she was sighing for the country, and for solitude; for the wide expanse of her own bright waves,—as she had called them,—and for the rocks of dear Portray. She had told Miss Macnulty and Augusta Fawn that she thirsted for the breezes of Ayrshire, so that she might return to her books and her thoughts. Amidst the whirl of London it was impossible either to read or to think. And she believed it, too,—herself. She so believed it, that on the first morning of her arrival she took a little volume

[1] Lord Fawn wishes to break off his engagement to Lizzie because of her refusal to give up the diamonds.

in her pocket, containing Shelley's 'Queen Mab', and essayed to go down upon the rocks. She had actually breakfasted at nine, and was out in the sloping grounds below the castle before ten, having made some boast to Miss Macnulty about the morning air.

She scrambled down,—not very far down, but a little way beneath the garden gate, to a spot on which a knob of rock cropped out from the scanty herbage of the incipient cliff. Fifty yards lower, the real rocks began; and, though the real rocks were not very rocky, not precipitous or even bold, and were partially covered with salt-fed mosses, down almost to the sea, nevertheless they justified her in talking about her rock-bound shore. The shore was hers,—for her life, and it was rockbound. This knob she had espied from her windows;—and, indeed, had been thinking of it for the last week, as a place appropriate to solitude and Shelley. She had stood on it before, and had stretched her arms with enthusiasm towards the just-visible mountains of Arran. On that occasion the weather, perhaps, had been cool; but now a blazing sun was overhead, and when she had been seated half a minute, and 'Queen Mab' had been withdrawn from her pocket, she found that it would not do. It would not do, even with the canopy she could make for herself with her parasol. So she stood up and looked about herself for shade;—for shade in some spot in which she could still look out upon 'her dear wide ocean, with its glittering smile.' For it was thus that she would talk about the mouth of the Clyde. Shelter near her there was none. The scrubby trees lay nearly half a mile to the right,—and up the hill, too. She had once clambered down to the actual shore, and might do so again. But she doubted that there would be shelter even there; and the clambering up on that former occasion had been a nuisance and would be a worse nuisance now. Thinking of all this, and feeling the sun keenly, she gradually retraced her steps to the garden within the moat, and seated herself, Shelley in hand, within the summer-house. The bench was narrow, hard, and broken; and there were some snails which discomposed her;—but, nevertheless, she would make the best of it. Her darling 'Queen Mab' must be read without the coarse, inappropriate, everyday surroundings of a drawing-room; and it was now manifest to her that, unless she could get up much earlier in the morning, or come out to her reading after sunset, the knob of rock would not avail her.

She began her reading, resolved that she would enjoy her poetry in spite of the narrow seat. She had often talked of 'Queen Mab', and perhaps she thought she had read it. This, however, was in truth her first attempt at that work. 'How wonderful is Death! Death and his brother, Sleep!' Then she half-closed the volume, and thought that she enjoyed the idea. Death,—and his brother Sleep! She did not know why they should be more wonderful than Action, or Life, or Thought;—but the words were of a nature which would enable her to remember them, and they would be good for quoting. 'Sudden arose Ianthe's soul; it stood all-beautiful in naked purity.' The name of Ianthe suited her exactly. And the antithesis conveyed to her mind by naked purity struck her strongly, and she determined to learn the passage by heart. Eight or nine lines were printed separately, like a stanza, and the labour would not be great, and the task, when done, would be complete. 'Instinct with inexpressible beauty and grace, Each stain of earthliness Had passed away, it reassumed Its native dignity, and stood Immortal amid ruin.' Which was instinct with beauty,—the stain or the soul, she did not stop to inquire, and may be excused for not understanding. 'Ah,'—she exclaimed to herself, 'how true it is; how one feels it; how it comes home to one!—"Sudden arose Ianthe's soul!"' And then she walked about the garden, repeating the words to herself, and almost forgetting the heat. ' "Each stain of earthliness had passed away." Ha;—yes. They will pass away, and become instinct with beauty and grace.' A dim idea came upon her that when this happy time should arrive, no one would claim her necklace from her, and that the man at the stables would not be so disagreeably punctual in sending in his bill. ' "All-beautiful in naked purity!" ' What a tawdry world was this, in which clothes and food and houses are necessary! How perfectly that boy-poet had understood it all! ' "Immortal amid ruin!" ' She liked the idea of the ruin almost as well as that of the immortality, and the stains quite as well as the purity. As immortality must come, and as stains were instinct with grace, why be afraid of ruin? But then, if people go wrong,—at least women,— they are not asked out any where! ' "Sudden arose Ianthe's soul; it stood all-beautiful—" ' And so the piece was learned, and Lizzie felt that she had devoted her hour to poetry in a quite rapturous manner.

The Eustace Diamonds, ch xxi

Here we have an expression of Trollope's anti-romanticism. Throughout the scene Lizzie's exciting and uplifting poetic illusions are satirically measured against prosaic fact. Her 'rocks' are tame, her 'sea' really only a river estuary. Her love of nature and solitude barely prevails over her physical discomfort and her dislike of snails. She sees herself as yearning (with Shelley) to escape from the restraints and cares of society into a state of nature, but she cannot envisage such a state except in familiar social terms: thus the phrase 'naked purity' to her conveys an 'antithesis', she assumes that it is Ianthe's 'stains' rather than her 'soul' that death renders 'instinct with beauty and grace', and she equates cosmic 'ruin' with social ostracism. Half-consciously, half-involuntarily, she is at war with reality itself: she aspires to 'act simplicity so well that the thing acted should be as powerful as the thing itself;—perhaps even more powerful'. But reality, as her reading of Shelley's poem shows, constantly asserts itself.

Trollope's satire, you will notice, is directed as much against Shelley as against Lizzie; and in the novel as a whole it presents Lizzie's romanticism as in most respects simply a magnified reflection of, and product of, that of society in general. Her illusions about herself are no more 'romantic'—perhaps even less so—than those which the sensation-hungry public invents (but half-believes) about her; and, against all the evidence, men rally to her support and palliate her offences in the name of a false, emptily romantic 'chivalry'. Like Melmotte (Extract 14), she is eventually 'exposed' and disgraced, but not before she has exposed society itself. And in a sense the final triumph is hers too, since her own faith in her romantic self is only strengthened by her worldly setbacks.

How subtle do you find Trollope's characterization of Lizzie here? Notice how, although he is for the most part reporting and commenting on Lizzie's thoughts—rather than representing them directly—he does achieve an effect very close to 'stream of consciousness' in his account of her reading of Shelley's lines.

The rogue hero

18

(*Mr. Scarborough has disinherited his wastrel elder son Mountjoy by asserting that he and Mountjoy's mother were not married when the child was born. Later, after his younger son Augustus has offended him, he reinstates Mountjoy by proving that he was, after all, born in wedlock.*)

He was a man who was from his constitution and heart capable of making great sacrifices for those he loved. He had a most thorough contempt for the character of an honest man. He did not believe in honesty, but only in mock honesty. And yet he would speak of an honest man with admiration, meaning something altogether different from the honesty of which men ordinarily spoke. The usual honesty of the world was with him all pretence, or, if not, assumed for the sake of the character it would achieve. Mr. Grey he knew to be honest; Mr. Grey's word he knew to be true; but he fancied that Mr. Grey had adopted this absurd mode of living with the view of cheating his neighbours by appearing to be better than others. All virtue and all vice were comprised by him in the words 'good-nature' and 'ill-nature'. All church-going propensities,—and these propensities in his estimate extended very widely,—he scorned from the very bottom of his heart. That one set of words should be deemed more wicked than another, as in regard to swearing, was to him a sign either of hypocrisy, of idolatry, or of feminine weakness of intellect. To women he allowed the privilege of being, in regard to thought, only something better than dogs. When his sister Martha shuddered at some exclamation from his mouth he would say to himself that she was a woman, not an idiot or a hypocrite. Of women, old and young, he had been very fond, and in his manner to them very tender; but when a woman rose to a way of thinking akin to his own, she was no longer a woman to his senses. Against such a one his taste revolted. She sank to the level of a man contaminated by petticoats. And law was hardly less absurd to him than religion. It consisted of a perplexed entanglement of rules got together so that the few might live in comfort at the expense of the many. Robbery, if you could get to the bottom of it, was bad, as was all violence; but taxation was robbery, rent was robbery, prices fixed according to the desire of the seller and not in obedience to justice, were robbery. 'Then you are the greatest of robbers,' his friends would say to him. He would admit it, allowing that in such a state of society he was not prepared to go out and live naked in the streets if he could help it. But he delighted to get the better of the law, and triumphed in his own iniquity, as has been seen by his conduct in reference to his sons.

In this way he lived, and was kind to many people, having a generous and an open hand. But he was a man who could hate with a bitter hatred, and he hated most those suspected by him of mean or dirty conduct. Mr. Grey, who constantly told him to his face that he was a rascal, he did not hate at all. Thinking Mr. Grey to be in some respects idiotic, he respected him, and almost loved him. He thoroughly believed Mr. Grey, thinking him to be an ass for telling so much truth unnecessarily. And he had loved his son Mountjoy in spite of all his iniquities, and had fostered him till it was impossible to foster him any longer. Then he had endeavoured to love Augustus, and did not in the least love him the less because his son told him frequently of the wicked things he had done. He did not object to be told of his wickedness even by his son. But Augustus suspected him of other things than those of which he accused him, and attempted to be sharp with him, and to get the better of him at his own game. And his son laughed at him and scorned him, regarded him as one who was troublesome only for a time, and who need not be treated with much attention, because he was there only for a time. Therefore he hated Augustus. But Augustus was his heir, and he knew that he must die soon.

But for how long could he live? And what could he yet do before he died? A braver man than Mr. Scarborough never lived,—that is, one who less feared to die. Whether that is true courage may be a question, but it was his, in conjunction with courage of another description. He did not fear to die, nor did he fear to live. But what he did fear was to fail before he died. Not to go out with the conviction that he was vanishing amidst the glory of success, was to him to be wretched at his last moment. And to be wretched at his last moment, or to anticipate that he should be so, was to him,—even so near his last hours,— the acme of misery. How much of life was left to him, so that he might recover something of success? Or was any moment left to him?

He could not sleep, so he rang his bell, and again sent for Mr. Merton. 'I have taken what you told me.'

'So best,' said Mr. Merton. For he did not always feel assured that this strange patient would take what had been ordered.

'And I have tried to sleep.'

'That will come after a while. You would not naturally sleep just after the tonic.'

'And I have been thinking of what you said about business. There is one thing I must do, and then I can remain quiet for a fortnight, unless I should be called upon to disturb my rest by dying.'

'We will hope not.'

'That may go as it pleases,' said the sick man. 'I want you now to write a letter for me to Mr. Grey.' Mr. Merton had undertaken to perform the duties of secretary as well as doctor, and had thought in this way to obtain some authority over his patient for the patient's own good. But he had found already that no authority had come to him. He now sat down at a table close to the bedside, and prepared to write in accordance with Mr. Scarborough's dictation. 'I think that Grey—the lawyer, you know—is a good man.'

'The world, as far as I hear it, says that he is honest.'

'I don't care a straw what the world says. The world says that I am dishonest, but I am not.' Merton could only shrug his shoulders. 'I don't care what you think. But I tell you a fact. I doubt whether Grey is so absolutely honest as I am, but as things go he is a good man.'

'Certainly.'

'But the world, I suppose, says that my son Augustus is honest.'

'Well, yes; I should suppose so.'

'If you have looked into him and have seen the contrary, I respect your intelligence.'

'I did not mean anything particular.'

'I dare say not, and if so, I mean nothing particular as to your intelligence. He, at any rate, is a scoundrel. Mountjoy,—you know Mountjoy?'

'Never saw him in my life.'

'I don't think he is a scoundrel,—not all round. He has

gambled when he has not had money to pay. That is bad.
And he has promised when he wanted money, and broken
his word as soon as he had got it; which is bad also. And
he has thought himself to be a fine fellow because he has
been intimate with lords and dukes, which is very bad. He
has never cared whether he paid his tailor. I do not mean
that he has merely got into debt, which a young man such
as he cannot help; but he has not cared whether his
breeches were his or another man's. That, too, is bad,
Though he has been passionately fond of women, it has
only only been for himself, not for the women, which is
very bad. There is an immense deal to be altered before he
can go to heaven.'

'I hope the change may come before it is too late,' said
Merton.

'These changes don't come very suddenly, you know.
But there is some chance for Mountjoy. I don't think that
there is any for Augustus!'

Mr. Scarborough's Family, ch. xxi

Unlike Lizzie Eustace, Mr. Scarborough is a conscious and
articulate critic of and rebel against conventional morality;
he also has a morality of his own, as we see in this passage.
What would you take to be Trollope's own attitude to Mr.
Scarborough and his morality?

It has been suggested that Trollope borrowed the idea for
Mr. Scarborough's Family—and for Mr. Scarborough himself—from the Jacobean drama. Certainly, both the story
and its chief character are far removed from 'commonplace
life'. They offer impressive proof of Trollope's ability to
make strange and improbable events seem quite normal
and unsurprising.

Violence

Physical violence—ranging from murder to horsewhipping and fisticuffs—is common in Trollope's novels. Usually, it is treated in such a calm and matter-of-fact way that he is often thought of as a 'quiet' novelist—one who practically ignores the more 'sensational' side of life. Frequently, too, the treatment is semi-comic, and in the sequel drama almost always gives way to anti-climax.

19

(*Mr. Kennedy, a man of great wealth but a fanatical puritan, suspects Phineas Finn—not without reason—of having alienated the affections of his wife.*)

'Let her come back to me, and she shall live in peace and quiet, and hear no word of reproach.'

'I can have nothing to do with it, Mr. Kennedy.'

'Then, sir, you shall abide my wrath.' With that he sprang quickly round, grasping at something which lay upon a shelf near him, and Phineas saw that he was armed with a pistol. Phineas, who had hitherto been seated, leaped to his legs; but the pistol in a moment was at his head, and the madman pulled at the trigger. But the mechanism of the instrument required that some bolt should be loosed before the hammer would fall upon the nipple, and the un-handy wretch for an instant fumbled over the work so that Phineas, still facing his enemy, had time to leap backwards towards the door. But Kennedy, though he was awkward, still succeeded in firing before our friend could leave the room. Phineas heard the thud of the bullet, and knew that it must have passed near his head. He was not struck, how-ever; and the man, frightened at his own deed, abstained from the second shot, or loitered long enough in his remorse to enable his prey to escape. With three or four steps Phineas leaped down the stairs, and, finding the front door closed, took shelter within Mrs. Macpherson's [*the land-lady's*] bar. 'The man is mad,' he said; 'did you not hear the shot?' The woman was too frightened to reply, but stood trembling, holding Phineas by the arm. There was nobody in the house, she said, but she and the two lasses. 'Nae doobt the Laird's by ordinaire,' she said at last. She had known of the pistol; but had not dared to have it removed. She and Macpherson had only feared that he would hurt himself,—and had at last agreed, as day after day passed without any injury from the weapon, to let the thing remain unnoticed. She had heard the shot, and had been sure that one of the two men above would have been killed.

Phineas was now in great doubt as to what duty was re-quired of him. His first difficulty consisted in this,—that his hat was still in Mr. Kennedy's room, and that Mrs. Mac-pherson altogether refused to go and fetch it. While they were still discussing this, and Phineas had not as yet resolved whether he would first get a policeman or go at once to Mr. Low [*a barrister*], the bell from the room was rung furiously. 'It's the Laird,' said Mrs. Macpherson, 'and if naebody waits on him he'll surely be shooting ane of us.' The two girls were now outside the bar shaking in their shoes, and evidently unwilling to face the danger. At last the door of the room above was opened, and our hero's hat was sent rolling down the stairs.

It was clear to Phineas that the man was so mad as to be not even aware of the act he had perpetrated. 'He'll do nothing more with the pistol,' he said, 'unless he should attempt to destroy himself.' At last it was determined that one of the girls should be sent to fetch Macpherson home from the Scotch Church, and that no application should be made at once to the police. It seemed that the Macphersons knew the circumstances of their guest's family, and that there was a cousin of his in London who was the only one with whom he seemed to have any near connection. The thing that had occurred was to be told to his cousin, and Phineas left his address, so that if it should be thought necessary he might be called upon to give his account of the affair. Then, in his perturbation of spirit, he asked for a glass of brandy; and having swallowed it, was about to take his leave. 'The brandy wull be saxpence, sir,' said Mrs. Macpherson, as she wiped the tears from her eyes.

Phineas Redux, ch. xxiii

Note here the ludicrous effect of Phineas's concern about his hat. Psychologically speaking, it is a subtle touch; but for Trollope, it also affords a means of bringing the excited reader abruptly down to earth and of ironically indicating the futility of violence, its irrelevance to ordinary life. A similar comic purpose is served by the Scotswoman Mrs. Macpherson's concern over her 'saxpence'.

As usual in his 'dramatic' scenes, Trollope concentrates on externals, achieving an effect of slightly absurd melodrama by temporarily disjoining acts from motives. His language and syntax are again worth studying closely: are they perhaps too restrained and orderly during his description of the murder attempt?

Tragedy

Though best known as a comic and satirical novelist, Trollope believed that the writer who can 'deal adequately with tragic elements is a greater artist and reaches a higher aim than the writer whose efforts never carry him above the mild walks of everyday life'. As you may already have sensed, his own prose-style and narrative methods do not naturally lend themselves to tragedy, which demands a more elevated, more 'poetic' view of human passion than his; but one or two of his characters do, in the intensity of their sufferings, achieve a pathos that is at least semi-tragic.

20

(*Louis Trevelyan has left his wife, and taken their young son to Italy, because he suspects her of having been unfaithful to him with Colonel Osborne. Bozzle is the private detective Trevelyan employed to 'spy' on his wife.*)

Thought deep, correct, continued, and energetic is quite

compatible with madness. At this time Trevelyan's mind
was so far unhinged, his ordinary faculties were so greatly
impaired, that they who declared him to be mad were justified in their declaration. His condition was such that the
happiness and welfare of no human being,—not even
his own,—could safely be entrusted to his keeping. He considered himself to have been injured by the world, to have
been the victim of so cruel a conspiracy among those who
ought to have been his friends, that there remained nothing
for him but to flee away from them and remain in solitude.
But yet, through it all, there was something approaching to
a conviction that he had brought his misery upon himself
by being unlike to other men; and he declared to himself
over and over again that it was better that he should suffer
than that others should be punished. When he was alone his
reflections respecting his wife were much juster than were
his words when he spoke either with her, or to others, of
her conduct. He would declare to himself not only that he
did not believe her to have been false to him, but that he
had never accused her of such a crime. He had demanded
from her obedience, and she had been disobedient. It had
been incumbent upon him,—so ran his own ideas, as expressed to himself in these long unspoken soliloquies,—to
exact obedience, or at least compliance, let the consequences be what they might. She had refused to obey or
even to comply, and the consequences were very grievous.
But, though he pitied himself with a pity that was feminine,
yet he acknowledged to himself that her conduct had been
the result of his own moody temperament. Every friend
had parted from him. All those to whose counsels he had
listened, had counselled him that he was wrong. The whole
world was against him. Had he remained in England, the
doctors and lawyers among them would doubtless have declared him to be mad. He knew all this, and yet he could
not yield. He could not say that he had been wrong. He
could not even think that he had been wrong as to the cause

of the great quarrel. He was one so miserable and so unfortunate,—so he thought,—that even in doing right he had fallen into perdition!

He had had two enemies, and between them they had worked his ruin. These were Colonel Osborne and Bozzle. It may be doubted whether he did not hate the latter the more strongly of the two. He knew now that Bozzle had been untrue to him, but his disgust did not spring from that so much as from the feeling that he had defiled himself by dealing with the man. Though he was quite assured that he had been right in his first cause of offence, he knew that he had fallen from bad to worse in every step that he had taken since. Colonel Osborne had marred his happiness by vanity, by wicked intrigue, by a devilish delight in doing mischief; but he, he himself, had consummated the evil by his own folly. Why had he not taken Colonel Osborne by the throat, instead of going to a low-born, vile, mercenary spy for assistance? He hated himself for what he had done; —and yet it was impossible that he should yield.

It was impossible that he should yield;—but it was yet open to him to sacrifice himself. He could not go back to his wife and say that he was wrong; but he could determine that the destruction should fall upon him and not upon her. If he gave up his child and then died,—died, alone, without any friend near him, with no word of love in his ears, in that solitary and miserable abode which he had found for himself,—then it would at least be acknowledged that he had expiated the injury that he had done. She would have his wealth, his name, his child to comfort her,—and would be troubled no longer by demands for that obedience which she had sworn at the altar to give him, and which she had since declined to render to him. Perhaps there was some feeling that the coals of fire would be hot upon her head when she should think how much she had received from him and how little she had done for him. And yet he loved her, with all his heart, and would even yet dream of bliss that might be possible with her,—had not the terrible hand of irresistible Fate come between them and marred it all. It was only a dream now. It could be no more than a dream. He put out his thin wasted hands and looked at them, and touched the hollowness of his own cheeks, and coughed that he might hear the hacking sound of his own infirmity, and almost took glory in his weakness. It could not be long before the coals of fire would be heaped upon her head. . . .

'There is a curse upon me,' said Trevelyan; 'it is written down in the book of my destiny that nothing shall ever love me!'

He went out from the house, and made his way down by the narrow path through the olives and vines to the bottom of the hill in front of the villa. It was evening now, but the evening was very hot, and though the olive trees stood in long rows, there was no shade. Quite at the bottom of the hill there was a little sluggish muddy brook, along the sides of which the reeds grew thickly and the dragon-flies were playing on the water. There was nothing attractive in the spot, but he was weary, and sat himself down on the dry hard bank which had been made by repeated clearing of mud from the bottom of the little rivulet. He sat watching the dragon-flies as they made their short flights in the warm air, and told himself that of God's creatures there was not one to whom less power of disporting itself in God's sun was given than to him. Surely it would be better for him that he should die, than live as he was now living without any of the joys of life. The solitude of Casalunga was intolerable to him, and yet there was no whither that he could go and find society. He could travel if he pleased. He had money at command, and, at any rate as yet, there was no embargo on his personal liberty. But how could he travel alone,—even if his strength might suffice for the work? There had been moments in which he had thought that he would be happy in the love of his child,—that the companionship of an infant would suffice for him if only the infant would love him. But all such dreams as that were over. To repay him for his tenderness his boy was always dumb before him. Louey would not prattle as he had used to do. He would not even smile, or give back the kisses with which his father had attempted to win him. In mercy to the boy he would send him back to his mother;—in mercy to the boy if not to the mother also. It was in vain that he should look for any joy in any quarter. Were he to return to England, they would say that he was mad!

He lay there by the brook-side till the evening was far advanced, and then he arose and slowly returned to the house. The labour of ascending the hill was so great to him that he was forced to pause and hold by the olive trees as he slowly performed his task. The perspiration came in profusion from his pores, and he found himself to be so weak that he must in future regard the brook as being beyond the tether of his daily exercise. Eighteen months ago he had been a strong walker, and the snow-bound paths of Swiss mountains had been a joy to him. He paused as he was slowly dragging himself on, and looked up at the wretched, desolate, comfortless abode which he called his home. Its dreariness was so odious to him that he was half-minded to lay himself down where he was, and let the night air come upon him and do its worst. In such case, however, some Italian doctor would be sent down who would say that he was mad. Above all things, and to the last, he must save himself from that degradation.

He Knew He Was Right, ch. lxxxiv

At one stage Trevelyan aptly compares himself to Othello, with Bozzle as his Iago. And his 'long unspoken soliloquies'—of which this passage is a sample—show him as a man with at least some of Othello's intelligence and imagination and with a good deal of Othello's tragic weakness for self-dramatization. His emotion, however, is passive, quiescent; he cannot find an outlet in violent action as Othello did, but can only do violence on himself—which he does, half-consciously, by behaving perversely, against his true inclinations. Trollope analyses his mind with remarkable perception and persistence, and as always makes brilliant use of externals—his gazing at his hands and touching of his hollow cheeks; the brook and the dragon-flies—to suggest the quality of his emotions. Indeed, the analysis is so intense and so psychologically convincing that we are barely aware of the narrator as coming between us and his subject. No doubt, despite Trollope's initial assurance, Trevelyan's thoughts are too 'deep, correct, [and] continued' even for the most methodical of crazed minds; but although the language and syntax hardly evoke the actual travail of a disordered mind, the travail of the author's imagination—the signs of *his* struggle to understand and define Trevelyan's mind in all its complexity—largely compensates.

Not the least of Trollope's claims to greatness as a novelist is his imaginative versatility, of which *He Knew He Was Right* and *Mr. Scarborough's Family* offer perhaps the most striking evidence. These two novels, along with some episodes in others, remind us that far from being merely the faithful and perceptive chronicler of mid-Victorian England he is also an explorer of remoter regions of the human spirit.

Bibliography

Trollope's Works

(WC=World's Classics edition, Oxford University Press, London and N.Y. O.p=WC edition at present—i.e. 1968 —out of print. Where no modern edition is listed, none exists. Novels that are recommended as offering the best introduction to Trollope's work are marked *.)

BARSETSHIRE NOVELS
   The Warden (1855), WC, 1918 etc.
   Barchester Towers (1857), WC, 1925 etc.
   Doctor Thorne (1858), WC, 1926 etc.
   Framley Parsonage (1861), WC, 1926 etc.
   The Small House at Allington (1864), WC, 1939 etc.
   The Last Chronicle of Barset (1867), WC, 1932 etc.

'PALLISER' (OR 'SEMI-POLITICAL') NOVELS
   Can You Forgive Her? (1864), WC, 1938 etc.
   Phineas Finn (1869), WC, 1937 etc.
   Phineas Redux (1874) WC, 1937 etc.
   The Prime Minister (1876), WC, 1938 etc.

The Duke's Children (1880), WC, 1938 etc.

OTHER NOVELS WITH ENGLISH SETTINGS
The Three Clerks (1858), WC, 1907 etc.
The Bertrams (1859)
Orley Farm (1862), WC, 1935 etc.
*Rachel Ray (1863), WC, 1924 etc. (o.p.)
Miss Mackenzie (1865), WC, 1924 etc. (o.p.)
The Belton Estate (1866), WC, 1923 etc.
*The Claverings (1867), WC, 1924 etc.
*He Knew He Was Right (1869), WC, 1948 etc.
*The Vicar of Bullhampton (1870), WC, 1924 etc.
The Struggles of Brown, Jones and Robinson (1870)
Sir Harry Hotspur of Humblethwaite (1871), WC, 1928
   etc. (o.p.)
*Ralph the Heir (1871), WC, 1939 etc. (o.p.)
*The Eustace Diamonds (1873), WC, 1930 etc.
Lady Anna (1874), WC, 1936 etc. (o.p.)
*The Way We Live Now (1875), WC, 1941 etc.
The American Senator (1877), WC, 1931 etc.
*Is He Popenjoy? (1878), WC, 1944 etc.
Cousin Henry (1879), WC, 1929 etc. (o.p.)
Dr. Wortle's School (1881), WC, 1928 etc.
Ayala's Angel (1881), WC, 1929 etc.
Kept in the Dark (1882)
Marion Fay (1882)
*Mr. Scarborough's Family (1883), WC, 1946 (o.p.)
An Old Man's Love (1884), WC, 1936 etc. (o.p.)

NOVELS WITH NON-ENGLISH SETTINGS
The Macdermots of Ballycloran (1847). Ireland.
The Kellys and the O'Kellys (1848), WC, 1929 etc. (o.p.)
   Ireland.

Castle Richmond (1860). Ireland.

An Eye for an Eye (1879), Anthony Blond, London, 1966;
Stein and Day, N.Y., 1967. Ireland.

The Landleaguers (1883). Ireland.

La Vendée (1850). France.

The Golden Lion of Granpère (1872), WC, 1946 (o.p.).
France.

Nina Balatka (1867), WC, 1946 etc. (with *Linda Tressel*
o.p.). Prague.

Linda Tressel (1868), WC, 1946 etc. *(with Nina Balatka)*.
Nuremberg.

Harry Heathcote of Gangoil (1874), Lansdowne Press,
Melbourne, 1963. Australia.

*John Caldigate (1879), WC, 1946 etc. (o.p.). Australia.

The Fixed Period (1882). 'Britannula'.

SHORT STORIES

Tales of All Countries (1861), WC, 1931 (o.p.)

Tales of All Countries; Second Series (1863)

Lotta Schmidt; and Other Stories (1867)

An Editor's Tales (1870)

*Why Frau Frohmann Raised Her Prices; and Other
Stories* (1882)

The Two Heroines of Plumplington (1882), Deutsch,
London, 1953; O.U.P., N.Y., 1954

(Also various other editions of single stories, and some
modern selections of stories.)

TRAVEL BOOKS

The West Indies and the Spanish Main (1859)

North America (1862), ed. D. Smalley and B. A. Booth,
Knopf, N.Y., 1951

Australia and New Zealand (1873), ed. P. D. Edwards and R. B. Joyce, Queensland University Press, Brisbane, 1967

South Africa (1878)

The Tireless Traveler, ed. B. A. Booth, University of California Press, Berkeley and Los Angeles, 1941

MISCELLANEOUS

An Autobiography (1883), WC, reset edition, 1953 etc.

The Letters of Anthony Trollope, ed. B. A. Booth, O.U.P., London and N.Y., 1951

Hunting Sketches (1865), Benn, London, 1952; John Day, N.Y., 1953

Travelling Sketches (1866)

Clergymen of the Church of England (1866)

The Commentaries of Caesar (1870)

How the 'Mastiffs' went to Iceland (1878)

Thackeray (1879)

The Life of Cicero (1880)

Lord Palmerston (1882)

The Noble Jilt (1850), Constable, London, 1923. Play.

Did He Steal It? (1869), Princeton University Library, N.J., 1952. Play.

London Tradesmen, Mathews and Marrot, London, 1927

Four Lectures, Constable, London, 1938

(Other, uncollected pieces are listed in Michael Sadleir, *Trollope; a Bibliography*, Constable, London, 1928.)

Some works about Trollope

HENRY JAMES, 'Anthony Trollope', reprinted in *The Art of Fiction and Other Essays*, O.U.P., N.Y., 1948, and *The*

House of Fiction, Hart-Davies, London, 1957: an early, and perceptive, critical essay.

T. H. S. ESCOTT, *Anthony Trollope; His Work, Associates, and Literary Originals*, John Lane, London, 1913: still useful as a biographical and literary-historical source, though gossipy and unreliable.

MARY L. IRWIN, *Anthony Trollope; a Bibliography*, H. W. Wilson, N.Y., 1926.

MICHAEL SADLEIR, *Trollope; a Commentary*, Constable, London and Houghton Mifflin, Boston, 1927; Oxford Paperback edition, London and N.Y., 1961: the most reliable biography; also contains criticism of varying quality.

MICHAEL SADLEIR, *Trollope; a Bibliography*, Constable, London, 1928.

L. P. and R. P. STEBBINS, *The Trollopes; the Chronicle of a Writing Family*, Columbia University Press, N.Y., 1945; Secker and Warburg, London, 1946: a stimulating but erratic critical biography, too apt to mistake psychoanalytic conjecture for fact.

A. O. J. COCKSHUT, *Anthony Trollope; a Critical Study*, Collins, London, 1955; Essential Books, N.Y., 1956: the best full-length criticism.

RAFAEL HELLING, *A Century of Trollope Criticism*, Helsinki, 1956: chiefly useful for extracts from and summaries of contemporary and posthumous studies of Trollope; not always accurate, and generalizations need to be treated with caution.

MARIO PRAZ, 'Anthony Trollope', *The Hero in Eclipse in Victorian Fiction*, O.U.P., London and N.Y., 1956: limited in scope, but perceptive.

BRADFORD A. BOOTH, *Anthony Trollope; Aspects of His Life and Art*, Indiana University Press, Bloomington, and Edward Hulton, London, 1958: a well documented but old-fashioned general survey.

HUGH SYKES DAVIES, *Trollope* ('British Book News' supplement), Longmans, London, 1960: a good short introduction with excellent bibliography.